IOSOP

Culture

STAFFROOM
EDITION

For information about schoolwide professional development, team training, or individual coaching in the application of Loving our Students on Purpose please contact:

- www.godwinconsulting.com.au
- admin@godwinconsulting.com.au

Editor: Allison Slack
Cover Design by Ashley Beck
Interior Design and Layout by Daniel Morales
ISBN: 978-0-6459046-7-3

DEDICATION

This book is dedicated to Northside Christian College, Brisbane, whose leadership have intentionally woven the heart of *Loving Our Students on Purpose* into the fabric of daily school life. Your steadfast pursuit of connection, joy, and responsibility is creating a culture where people feel seen, valued, and empowered — a living example of what it means to lead with purpose.

Books

Loving our Students on Purpose
Cultural Architect (coming 2026)

LoSoP Momentum Series

(Weekly aligned foundational philosophy of Loving our Students on Purpose)
Staffroom Edition--book, ebook, or video series available
Future editions coming soon!

LoSoP Culture Series

(Weekly aligned foundational values to build a Culture of Love)
Boardroom Edition
Staffroom Edition
Primary Classroom Edition
Secondary Classroom Edition
Family Room Edition

Podcasts

Loving Our Students on Purpose Journey Podcast
Culture Daily: Education Edition

Resources Available

www.godwinconsulting.com.au
Explore our full range of LoSoP resources designed to bring connection and joyful responsibility into everyday practice—from Desk Flips, Printable Poster Collections, and Flash Cards to Online Courses, Bookmarks, and more.

For bulk purchases email admin@godwinconsulting.com.au

TABLE OF CONTENTS

BUILDING A CULTURE OF LOVE

Welcome to the LoSoP Culture Series: Staffroom Edition

Creating Staffrooms Where Every Person Feels Beloved, Chosen, and Cherished

This series is your invitation to create something lasting in your school: a culture of love where every staff member feels beloved, chosen, and cherished. Whether you're leading the team or simply showing up each day to make a difference, this resource is designed to help you build trust, grow in shared ownership, restore relationships, and strengthen the culture you carry together.

The *LoSoP Culture Series* is built on a simple but powerful truth: love changes everything. I don't mean the fluffy or feel-good kind of love, but the kind of love that shows up with boundaries, grace, and purpose––the kind of love that holds space for challenge, speaks the truth kindly, and helps staff and students alike learn how to restore connection when things go wrong.

Across 40 weekly sessions, your team will reflect on the culture you're creating together. Each session focuses on one principle of connection, drawn from four foundational pillars: *Healthy Relationships, Joyful Responsibility, Genuine Restoration,* and *Leadership Development.*

This series has been intentionally designed to align with the same weekly focus used in classrooms, boardrooms, and family homes. That means your staff, students, and families can all be growing in the same direction--learning a shared language of connection, safety, and responsibility across every part of the school community.

What Is a Culture of Love?

A culture of love doesn't happen by accident—it's created on purpose. It's formed in the way we speak to each other, how we handle mistakes, how we set boundaries, and how we build trust through everyday moments.

This series is guided by four core truths:

1. Our goal is connection.
2. Love is a powerful choice.
3. Fear is the enemy of connection.
4. Building and protecting connection is a learning journey.

Each week, you'll come back to these truths as you reflect, connect, and lead forward together.

The Four Pillars of Staff Culture of Love

Every session explores one or more of the four pillars that shape a healthy school culture:

- Healthy Relationships--where all staff feel safe, seen, and supported.

- Joyful Responsibility--where shared ownership leads to collective strength.
- Genuine Restoration--where honesty, grace, and repair are part of everyday life.
- Leadership Development--where every staff member is empowered to lead from where they are.

These pillars will help you shape a staffroom culture where connection is the norm, not the exception, and where everyone contributes to the emotional tone of the school.

How to Use This Series

Use it during staff meetings, in professional learning groups, or in smaller connect groups. Each session includes a key idea, reflection prompts, and a practical step to try during the week. There's also space at the end of each session for personal reflection in your Growth Journal.

This isn't about ticking a box--it's about building a staff culture where people feel safe to be human and supported to grow.

Why It Matters

Staff culture isn't a side note—it's the foundation. The way we treat each other shapes how we treat our students. When connection is strong among staff, everything flows more smoothly—collaboration, well-being, communication, and trust.

This series will help your team create a culture where love isn't just talked about--it's lived.

This is a staffroom built on love—on purpose.

A NOTE FROM BERNII

Dear Team,

Welcome to the *LoSoP Culture Series: Staffroom Edition*—a resource created to support you as you build the kind of culture that makes your school feel like a place where people truly belong.

If you've worked in a school for any length of time, you know this work is more than policies, programs, posters or planning meetings. It's relational. It's emotional. It's human. The way we treat each other—in the corridors, in the classroom, and yes, in the staffroom—shapes the entire culture our students walk into each day.

This series is an opportunity to pause together once a week and talk about what really matters: connection, responsibility, restoration, and the kind of leadership that comes from the inside out. It's a chance to reflect honestly, speak openly, and grow personally—while supporting one another as we do.

You'll explore big ideas through real conversations:

- How do we build trust when we're under pressure?
- How do we repair connection when we've been hurt or misunderstood?
- How do we lead ourselves with integrity when the day feels hard?

These aren't just professional skills. They're life skills. And they're worth investing in—for ourselves, for each other, and for the students watching us every day.

Creating a culture of love doesn't mean we'll get it right all the time. But it does mean we keep showing up—willing to learn, to listen, and to lead with care.

Thank you for choosing to be part of a staff culture that values people over performance, presence over perfection, and love over fear. The way you show up for your students and your colleagues is shaping something powerful.

I'm so grateful you're on the journey. And I'm cheering you on every step of the way.

With heart,
Bernii

HOW TO USE THIS SERIES— STAFFROOM EDITION

Creating Staffrooms Where Every Person Feels Valued, Seen, and Connected

The *LoSoP Culture Series: Staffroom Edition* is a practical, flexible tool designed to help your team build a culture of love—where connection is intentional, responsibility is shared, restoration is normal, and leadership is something everyone can grow in.

Each session offers a short, focused conversation to strengthen your staff culture. It's not about adding pressure—it's about creating meaningful moments that support the people behind the roles.

This edition aligns with the weekly topics in the Classroom, Boardroom, and Family Room editions, so your whole school community can be growing in the same direction at the same time.

What's Inside Each Session

Quote of the Week

A short phrase beginning with "In a culture of love…" to set the tone. Read it together to start your session with shared intention.

Discuss

Use the questions to guide a conversation with your whole team or a smaller group. These are designed to invite open reflection about your staff culture and how you interact with students, colleagues, and families.

Learn

Here you'll find the key idea explained in simple language. This helps everyone understand why it matters and how it connects to real-life school settings.

Demonstrate

These are optional activities to help bring the concept to life. You'll find short games, partner tasks, or examples to try together. Feel free to adapt these or come up with your own. They're meant to be flexible and fun.

Leader Share

The session host shares a short personal reflection—a story, lesson, or insight that ties to the week's focus. It doesn't need to be polished, just real. Going first creates safety and helps others open up.

Our School Statement

Write a short sentence together that begins with: "In this school..." This captures your shared belief for the week and can be written on a whiteboard, poster, or shared doc as a reminder. Remember that everyone needs to agree on one core statement, and that you will be collecting these for the final activity in Week 40.

Connect Groups

Break into small groups of 3–4 people to reflect more personally using the Connect Group questions. These groups are where trust grows. Keep the same group for the whole year to build consistency and depth. Rotate who shares first each week, and encourage everyone to participate.

My Goal This Week

Everyone writes one small, specific action they'll take that week to put the learning into practice. This might be something like offering a colleague a listening ear, apologising well, or showing appreciation.

Personal Growth Reflection

At the end of the week, staff are invited to reflect privately. Use the questions provided to check in on your personal growth and notice where the learning showed up.

Making the Most of These Sessions

- **Set Up Connect Groups** early in the term—3 or 4 people per group. Stick with the same group across the year to build trust and depth.
- **Create a Leader Roster** so everyone knows when they're leading. Share a simple schedule so the facilitator has time to read ahead, prepare their story or demo, and feel confident hosting.

- **Encourage Participation** but allow for different comfort levels. Staff can engage in the way that feels safe to them, but over time, everyone should feel seen and included.

- **Be Creative with Demonstrations.** The ideas provided are just a starting point—feel free to make them your own. Use something that suits your team's culture and energy.

- **Have Fun.** These sessions are a chance to connect, reflect, and build something beautiful together. Keep it light where needed, go deeper when it's right, and enjoy the journey.

Time-Friendly Format

Each session takes around 10–20 minutes and can be used:

- As a staff meeting opener
- In a weekly well-being or team-building slot
- As part of leadership or year-level team time

You can also stretch a session over two weeks if more time is needed to reflect or explore the concept fully.

Final Thoughts

Great school culture doesn't come from policies or posters, it comes from people––people who choose to show up, reflect honestly, and grow together.

These sessions are here to support you in doing just that.

TOP TIP

GET READY WITH A
FEELINGS WHEEL

Before you begin the *LoSoP Culture* Series, we recommend printing a large feelings wheel poster and displaying it in your environment. You can find a variety of feelings wheels online by simply googling "Feelings Wheel"—choose one that suits the age group you're working with.

You may observe that topics in this series include a "How do you feel?" question. It's important to focus on our own experiences, rather than asking, "How did that make you feel?" which can unintentionally place the responsibility for feelings outside the person. By asking "How do you feel?", we support each other to take ownership of our own internal emotional experiences.

Encourage participants to move beyond basic labels like *sad, bad, mad,* or *glad*, and instead explore the feelings wheel to identify a more specific emotion. This simple practice helps expand their emotional vocabulary and builds their capacity to express themselves with clarity and confidence––an essential skill for connection, empathy, and self-awareness.

All emotions are good. They exist to signal that action is needed. Sometimes emotions reveal that a boundary has been crossed and invite us to take responsibility for how we protect our future boundaries. At other times they highlight a need that requires attention, or they expose a fear that has been triggered. Emotions can also be a signal that something deserves to be celebrated. Whatever the emotion, it is doing its job of communicating. Our task is to listen well and respond with wisdom.

PART ONE

CULTIVATING HEALTHY RELATIONSHIPS IN OUR STAFF CULTURE

Leadership starts with connection.

In this first part of the series, we focus on laying the foundations for a staff culture built on trust, respect, and strong relationships. In every school, it's the staff—not just the leadership team—who set the tone for how connection is felt in the halls, in the classrooms, and across the community.

Healthy relationships at work don't happen by accident—they happen on purpose. They're shaped in the way we greet one another, how we respond in moments of pressure, how we resolve misunderstandings, and how we show up with kindness and accountability.

This section of the series invites staff to grow together in the everyday habits that create emotional safety and belonging—the kind of culture where people feel supported, valued, and connected. Whether you've worked together for years or just met this term, these sessions will help your team build deeper trust and stronger communication.

Staff culture sets the tone for student culture. When we invest in healthy relationships with each other, it flows naturally into how we teach, lead, and support students.

Let's start by building connection—with intention, with compassion, and with love.

WEEK 1:

LISTENING THAT BUILDS TRUST AND CONNECTION

*"In a culture of love, listening means creating space
for every voice to matter."*

Discuss:

- What does listening mean to us in this school?
- What does it look like when we truly listen to students, colleagues, and parents?
- What does listening *not* look like?

Learn:

Listening is one of the most powerful ways we build connection. When people feel heard, they feel valued. Listening is not just about waiting for our turn to speak—it's about seeking to understand before we respond. In a noisy world, listening is a radical act of love.

Demonstrate:

A practical way to demonstrate this is to play a quick game of "Chinese Whispers" (also known as "Telephone"). Ask staff to form a circle or line. Start a message at one end and pass it quietly from person to person. Make up your own message or use this one: "If you've ever visited Grandma on a Thursday, you'd know she is probably baking cherry pie and listening to Doris Day reruns on the radio while Grandpa can be heard snoring from his recliner in the den."

Reflect together on how listening carefully affects the clarity of communication. Discuss how small distractions or assumptions can alter what is heard and understood.

Alternatively, invite staff to pair up and practise active listening by sharing for 2 minutes each without interruption, while their partner listens deeply and then reflects back what they heard.

Leader Share:

As the host of this session, share a moment from your own experience where listening made all the difference—or where a missed opportunity to listen became a lesson. What did it teach you about the power of slowing down, creating space, and truly hearing the heart behind the words?

Our School Statement:

Together, write your school statement for the week.

For example: *"In this school, we listen with our hearts—because every voice matters."*

In this school,

Connect Groups:

- Share a time when you felt truly listened to. What made it powerful?
- What can get in the way of listening well in our school environment?
- What could we do this week to slow down and listen more deeply to students or each other?

My Goal This Week:

Write one small, specific action you can take to practise listening well. It might be slowing down, asking clarifying questions, or giving someone your full attention.

Personal Growth Reflection:

- Where did I practise listening well this week?
- What challenged me about listening?
- How did listening impact my relationships?
- Where do I want to keep growing in listening well next week?

WEEK 2:

GIVING AND RECEIVING FEEDBACK WITH COURAGE AND CARE

"In a culture of love, feedback means we care enough to speak the truth and listen with humility."

Discuss:

- What does healthy feedback look like in our staff culture?
- What makes giving feedback hard?
- What makes receiving feedback hard?

Learn:

Feedback is not about criticism or control. In a healthy culture, feedback is a gift we give to help others grow. It requires courage to speak with honesty and kindness, and it requires humility to listen without defensiveness. When feedback is part of our everyday staff culture, we create a safe place for growth, learning, and connection.

Demonstrate:

Draw a large number 6 on one side of a piece of paper or whiteboard and a 9 on the opposite side, so that depending on where you stand, you see either a 6 or a 9.

Invite two volunteers to stand on either side and argue their view of what number they see. After some discussion, ask them to swap sides to see the other person's perspective.

Discuss together:

- What happens when we only see our perspective?
- How does this demonstration remind us of the importance of curiosity, feedback, and understanding?

Feedback works best when we take time to understand the other person's view and stay open to learning and connection.

Leader Share:

As the host of this session, share a time when feedback helped you grow or a time when giving feedback required courage and care. What did you learn from the experience?

Our School Statement:

Together, write your school statement for the week.

For example: *"In this school, we give feedback with kindness and receive it with humility."*

In this school,

Connect Groups:

- Share a time when feedback helped you grow.
- What does giving feedback with kindness look like in our school?
- How can we practise receiving feedback with humility this week?

My Goal This Week:

Write one small, specific action you can take to practise giving or receiving feedback well.

Personal Growth Reflection:

- Where did I practise giving or receiving feedback well this week?
- What challenged me about feedback?
- How did feedback impact my relationships or professional growth?
- Where do I want to keep growing next week?

WEEK 3:

EMPATHY—UNDERSTANDING BEFORE RESPONDING

"In a culture of love, empathy means we seek to understand before we respond."

Discuss:

- What does empathy look like in our staff culture?
- What is the difference between empathy and sympathy?
- What happens when we respond before understanding?

Learn:

Empathy is the ability to step into someone else's world and see things from their perspective. It doesn't mean fixing their problem or feeling sorry for them. It means pausing long enough to understand their experience, feelings, or challenges. Empathy builds trust because it communicates: "You matter. Your story matters."

In our staff culture, empathy helps us listen without judgement, respond with kindness, and support one another with understanding.

Demonstrate:

Use two chairs placed back-to-back to represent disconnection. Invite two people to sit on the chairs, facing away from each other. Ask them to share something simple (like describing their morning) while not being able to see each other. Then invite them to move their chairs to face one another. Reflect together:

- How does being face-to-face change the interaction?
- What does this show us about empathy?

Empathy is choosing to turn towards others, rather than staying distant or disengaged.

Leader Share:

As the host of this session, share a story of when someone showed you empathy and it made a difference—or a time when you learnt the importance of slowing down to understand someone's experience before responding.

Our School Statement:

Together, write your school statement for the week.

For example: *"In this school, we choose empathy by seeking to understand before we respond."*

In this school,

Connect Groups:

- Share a time when empathy made a difference in your life.
- What can get in the way of showing empathy in our school environment?
- What could we each do this week to practise empathy with students, staff, or families?

My Goal This Week:

Write one small, specific action you can take to practise empathy well.

Personal Growth Reflection:

- Where did I practise empathy well this week?
- What challenged me about showing empathy?
- How did empathy impact my relationships or staff culture?
- Where do I want to keep growing next week?

WEEK 4:

SPEAKING WITH KINDNESS TO CREATE A SAFE CULTURE

*"In a culture of love, kindness means using
our words to build, not break."*

Discuss:

- What does speaking with kindness look like in our staff culture?

- Why is it important to create safety with our words?

- What happens when kindness is missing from our conversations?

Learn:

Kindness is not weakness. Kindness is strength under control. The words we speak create the atmosphere in our teams and classrooms.

Kind words build connection, safety, and respect. Unkind words, sarcasm, or thoughtless comments can quickly damage trust and create fear.

In a healthy staff culture, we choose our words carefully, speak life over one another, and create safe spaces for growth.

Demonstrate:

Bring a small jar of glitter or sand to represent words. Pour the glitter slowly onto a dark cloth to show how words leave a lasting impression—for better or worse. Once words are spoken, they can't be taken back. Reflect together:

- What kind of words do we want to leave behind?
- How can our words create safety and connection?

Leader Share:

As the host of this session, share a story of when someone's words built you up or created safety for you. Or share a time when unkind words impacted you or someone else, and what you learned from that experience.

Our School Statement:

Together, write your school statement for the week.

For example: *"In this school, we use our words to build up, not break down."*

In this school,

Connect Groups:

- Share a time when someone's words made a positive impact on you.
- What does it look like to use words that build in our staff environment?
- How can we create a culture where kindness is normal and expected?

My Goal This Week:

Write one small, specific action you can take to practise speaking with kindness this week.

Personal Growth Reflection:

- Where did I practise speaking with kindness this week?
- What challenged me about using kind words?
- How did kindness impact my relationships or staff culture?
- Where do I want to keep growing next week?

WEEK 5:

SOLVING PROBLEMS TOGETHER AS A TEAM

"In a culture of love, solving problems means working together with honesty, respect, and creativity."

Discuss:

- What does healthy problem-solving look like in our staff culture?
- What happens when we avoid problems or try to fix them alone?
- What is the benefit of solving problems together?

Learn:

Every school will face problems—big and small. What defines our culture is not whether we have problems, but how we choose to approach them. Healthy teams bring problems to the table early. They listen well, seek to understand all perspectives, and work together to find solutions.

Problem-solving is not about blame or control. It's about collaboration, creativity, and responsibility.

Demonstrate:

Bring a large knot of string, yarn, or rope. Invite a few staff to untangle the knot together while the rest of the group observes. Prior to the demonstration, arrange for one or two staff members to hackle and give "back-seat" advice from the sidelines. Reflect together:

- What helped the team succeed?
- What got in the way?
- How does this represent our approach to problem-solving?

Healthy problem-solving happens when we listen, work together, and stay patient.

Leader Share:

As the host of this session, share a story of when a problem was solved well in your school or workplace because of teamwork. Or share a lesson you learned from a situation that was not solved well, and what you would do differently now.

Our School Statement:

Together, write your school statement for the week.

For example: *"In this school, we solve problems together with honesty, respect, and creativity."*

In this school,

Connect Groups:
- Share a time when you experienced great teamwork in solving a problem.
- What helps us bring problems to the table early in our staff culture?
- How can we practise solving problems together this week?

My Goal This Week:
Write one small, specific action you can take to practise solving problems well with others this week.

Personal Growth Reflection:
- Where did I practise solving problems together this week?
- What challenged me about collaborative problem-solving?
- How did solving problems together impact our staff culture?
- Where do I want to keep growing next week?

WEEK 6:

RESPECT—THE FOUNDATION OF A THRIVING WORKPLACE

"In a culture of love, respect means treating every person with value, dignity, and care."

Discuss:

- What does respect look like in our staff culture?
- How do we show respect to students, families, and one another?
- What happens when respect is missing in a workplace?

Learn:

Respect is the starting point for every healthy relationship. It's not something people have to earn; it's something we choose to give because every person has inherent value.

Respect shows up in how we listen, how we speak, and how we act towards others—especially when we disagree or when tensions are high.

In our school, respect sets the tone for how we work together, build trust, and create a culture where everyone can thrive.

Demonstrate:

Bring two different-sized containers or boxes. Place a small, fragile item (an egg would work great) in each. In one, pack it carefully with padding; in the other, leave it loose. Shake both gently (or go for it and give it a good shake). Reflect together:

- Which item was better protected?
- What does this show us about how respect protects relationships?

Respect is like the padding around fragile things––it keeps people safe enough to grow and contribute fully.

Leader Share:

As the host of this session, share a story of when you felt respected and how it impacted you, or a time when disrespect created disconnection and what you learned from that experience.

Our School Statement:

Together, write your school statement for the week.

For example: *"In this school, we show respect to everyone in our words, actions, and attitudes."*

In this school,

Connect Groups:

- Share a time when you felt deeply respected in your work or personal life.
- What small things show respect in our staff environment?
- How can we practise showing respect this week?

My Goal This Week:

Write one small, specific action you can take to practise respect well this week.

Personal Growth Reflection:

- Where did I practise showing respect well this week?
- What challenged me about showing respect?
- How did respect impact my relationships or staff culture?
- Where do I want to keep growing next week?

WEEK 7:

BETTER TOGETHER—BUILDING A COLLABORATIVE TEAM CULTURE

"In a culture of love, together means we value connection over isolation and teamwork over competition."

Discuss:

- What does working better together look like in our staff culture?

- What challenges can get in the way of teamwork?

- What are the benefits of working together rather than working alone?

Learn:

We were never meant to do this work alone. Healthy school cultures are built on strong teams who know how to collaborate, communicate, and care for one another. Being "better together" means recognising that everyone has something valuable to contribute.

It also means we intentionally include, encourage, and look out for one another. We create a culture where no one is left behind and every voice matters.

Demonstrate:

Bring a set of sticks or pencils. Try to break a single stick easily—it snaps quickly. Then hold a large bundle of sticks together and try to break them. Reflect together:

- What does this show us about teamwork?
- How does unity strengthen us?

Better together means stronger, safer, and more supported.

Leader Share:

As the host of this session, share a story of when you experienced great teamwork and connection in a workplace. What made it powerful? Or share a time when isolation or competition damaged teamwork, and what you learned.

Our School Statement:

Together, write your school statement for the week.

For example: *"In this school, we work together, include others, and value every contribution."*

In this school,

Connect Groups:

- Share a time when you experienced great teamwork.

- What small actions help build a collaborative staff culture?

- How can we practise working better together this week?

My Goal This Week:

Write one small, specific action you can take to practise teamwork or collaboration well this week.

Personal Growth Reflection:

- Where did I practise teamwork or collaboration well this week?

- What challenged me about working with others?

- How did collaboration impact our staff culture?

- Where do I want to keep growing next week?

WEEK 8:

BUILDING TRUST—THE BRIDGE THAT HOLDS US

"In a culture of love, trust means showing up consistently with honesty, integrity, and care."

Discuss:

- What does trust look like in our staff culture?
- What behaviours build trust over time?
- What behaviours break trust quickly?

Learn:

Trust is the invisible bridge that holds teams together. It takes time to build, but only moments to damage. Trust grows through small, consistent actions—being reliable, honest, respectful, and caring.

In our school, trust is built when we do what we say we will do, speak truth with kindness, and take responsibility for our actions. Trust allows us to feel safe, take risks, and work together with confidence.

Demonstrate:

Create a simple bridge using building blocks or cardboard between two objects. Show how strong the bridge is when built carefully and consistently. Then remove or weaken some pieces (representing dishonesty, gossip, or broken promises). Reflect together:

- What makes trust strong?
- What weakens or breaks trust?

Trust is built slowly and intentionally but lost quickly without care.

Leader Share:

As the host of this session, share a story of when trust was built well in a team you were part of, or a time when trust was broken and what you learned from that experience.

Our School Statement:

Together, write your school statement for the week.

For example: *"In this school, we build trust through consistency, honesty, and care."*

In this school,

Connect Groups:

- Share a time when you experienced high trust in a team.

- What small actions help build trust in our staff culture?

- How can we practise building trust this week?

My Goal This Week:

Write one small, specific action you can take to build trust well this week.

Personal Growth Reflection:

- Where did I practise building trust well this week?

- What challenged me about building or protecting trust?

- How did trust impact our staff relationships or culture?

- Where do I want to keep growing next week?

WEEK 9:

RESPONSIBLE AND CONNECTED— LEADING OURSELVES WELL

"In a culture of love, responsibility means owning my actions while staying connected in relationship."

Discuss:

- What does responsibility look like in our staff culture?
- Why is it important to stay connected while taking responsibility?
- What happens when responsibility turns into blame or control?

Learn:

Healthy responsibility means owning my choices, words, and actions—not someone else's. In a thriving staff culture, responsibility is paired with connection. We lead ourselves well without disconnecting from others, even when mistakes happen.

Being responsible is not about controlling people. It's about leading ourselves with integrity and creating a culture where everyone is empowered to do the same.

Demonstrate:

Using butcher's paper, create a target with two circles, one inside the other (IMPORTANT: You will need these targets for the activity in Week 14, so keep them handy). Label the inside circle "My Responsibility" and the outside circle "Not My Responsibility." Invite staff to write different situations or behaviours on sticky notes and decide which circle they belong in. Reflect together:

- What happens when we step outside our circle of responsibility?
- How does staying in our circle help us stay connected?

Healthy teams know what belongs to them and what doesn't.

Leader Share:

As the host of this session, share a story of when you learned the importance of owning your responsibility without trying to control others. What did this teach you about leadership or connection?

Our School Statement:

Together, write your school statement for the week.

For example: *"In this school, we lead ourselves well and stay connected in every relationship."*

In this school,

Connect Groups:

- Share a time when taking responsibility strengthened a relationship.
- What helps us stay in our own circle of responsibility?
- How can we practise responsible leadership this week?

My Goal This Week:

Write one small, specific action you can take to practise leading yourself well this week.

Personal Growth Reflection:

- Where did I practise responsible leadership well this week?
- What challenged me about staying connected while taking responsibility?
- How did responsibility impact our staff culture?
- Where do I want to keep growing next week?

WEEK 10:

CREATING SUPPORTIVE STAFF FRIENDSHIPS USING THE EMPOWERMENT MODEL

"In a culture of love, friendship means we champion one another and help each other grow."

Discuss:

- What does a supportive friendship look like in our staff culture?
- How can friendships at work positively impact well-being and growth?
- What happens when friendships become unhealthy or exclusive?

Learn:

Supportive friendships in the workplace are powerful. They create belonging, safety, and encouragement—but also accountability and honesty. The Empowerment Model reminds us that strong friendships include empathy, boundaries, truth-telling, and celebration.

Healthy friendships help us become better people, not just more comfortable people.

The Empowerment Model includes:

- **Empathy**: I listen and understand.
- **Empower**: I believe in your ability to grow.
- **Explore**: I ask curious questions.
- **Educate**: I share what might help.
- **Expect**: I hold you accountable.
- **Encourage**: I celebrate your progress.

Demonstrate:

Arrange for a role-play demonstration with another staff member. Set up a scenario where one person is facing a challenge in a friendship or work scenario.

Leader Share:

As the host of this session, share a story of when you used the Empowerment Model to support a student, colleague, or parent. What difference did it make?

Our School Statement:

Together, write your school statement for the week.

For example: *"In this school, we build supportive friendships that help each other grow."*

In this school,

Connect Groups:

- Share a time when a friendship helped you grow.
- What does the Empowerment Model teach us about supporting friends well?
- How can we practise supportive friendships this week?

My Goal This Week:

Write one small, specific action you can take to practise being a supportive friend this week.

Personal Growth Reflection:

- Where did I practise supportive friendship well this week?
- What challenged me about empowering others?
- How did supportive friendships impact our staff culture?
- Where do I want to keep growing next week?

SECTION TWO

BUILDING JOYFUL RESPONSIBILITY IN OUR WORK AND LEADERSHIP

Ownership with encouragement creates momentum.

In this section, we turn our attention to how responsibility is carried within our staff culture—not as a burden, but as something that can be shared with joy and purpose.

Joyful responsibility means we take ownership of our choices, our contribution, and our impact—while also recognising that we are part of a team. It's not about perfection or pressure. It's about showing up with integrity, making space for one another, and supporting each other through the ups and downs of school life.

When responsibility is embraced with encouragement and trust, staff begin to feel empowered rather than exhausted. Work becomes more purposeful. Collaboration becomes more meaningful. And leadership becomes something everyone can practise, no matter their title or role.

This section invites staff to reflect on how we manage our time, support each other, keep our word, and hold high expectations for ourselves without losing compassion. It's about creating a staff culture where doing our best doesn't come at the cost of our well-being, and where shared responsibility leads to shared success.

WEEK 11:

OWNING YOUR ACTIONS AND PROFESSIONAL IMPACT

"In a culture of love, ownership means taking responsibility for my choices, my attitude, and my contribution to this workplace."

Discuss:

- What does owning our actions look like in our staff culture?
- What happens when we avoid responsibility?
- How does personal ownership impact team culture?

Learn:

Ownership is a mark of professionalism and leadership. It means I choose to lead myself first, take responsibility for my words and actions, and own my role in creating a positive staff culture.

When we own our actions, we stop blaming, avoid gossip, and create solutions. We influence culture by what we bring to every conversation, meeting, and classroom.

Ownership says: "If I see it, I can do something about it."

Demonstrate:

Place a mirror in front of the group. Reflect together:

- Who is responsible for my attitude, words, and actions?
- What does the mirror remind me about ownership?

True ownership starts with the person in the mirror.

Leader Share:

As the host of this session, share a story of when owning your actions changed a situation for the better, or when avoiding responsibility made things harder. What did you learn?

Our School Statement:

Together, write your school statement for the week.

For example: *"In this school, we own our actions and lead ourselves with integrity."*

In this school,

Connect Groups:

- Share a time when taking ownership improved a situation.

- What does personal ownership look like in our school?

- How can we practise owning our actions and impact this week?

My Goal This Week:

Write one small, specific action you can take to practise ownership well this week.

Personal Growth Reflection:

- Where did I practise ownership well this week?

- What challenged me about taking responsibility?

- How did ownership impact our staff culture?

- Where do I want to keep growing next week?

WEEK 12:

POWERFUL PEOPLE BUILD POWERFUL TEAMS

"In a culture of love, powerful people lead themselves well, take ownership of their actions, and create space for others to thrive."

Discuss:

- What does it mean to be a powerful person in our staff culture?
- How do powerful people build strong teams?
- What happens when people act powerless in the workplace?

Learn:

Being powerful is not about control—it's about responsibility. Powerful people lead themselves first. They stay calm under pressure, take ownership of their attitude, and create solutions rather than problems.

There are three key characteristics of powerful people:

1. They require respectful relationships—they won't stay in unhealthy dynamics or tolerate disrespect.

2. They set limits and boundaries—because they value themselves and know their role.

3. They manage themselves regardless of what others are doing—their behaviour is not dependent on someone else's actions.

Powerful people help build powerful teams because they model what it looks like to stay responsible, respectful, and connected—even in difficult situations.

Powerless behaviour shows up as blame, avoidance, controlling others, or waiting for someone else to fix a problem.

Powerful staff create an environment where everyone can bring their best.

Demonstrate:

Create two simple signs: "Powerful Person" and "Powerless Person." Invite staff to brainstorm behaviours or language that would fit each category. Discuss:

- What habits do we want to grow?
- What habits do we need to change?

Choosing powerful behaviour grows healthy culture.

Leader Share:

As the host of this session, share a story of when you recognised the difference between powerful and powerless behaviour in yourself or others. What did it teach you about leading well?

Our School Statement:

Together, write your school statement for the week.

For example: *"In this school, we choose powerful behaviour that builds a strong team."*

In this school,

Connect Groups:

- Share a time when you stayed powerful in a difficult situation.
- Which of the three characteristics of powerful people do you find easiest? Hardest?
- How can we practise staying powerful and leading ourselves well this week?

My Goal This Week:

Write one small, specific action you can take to practise powerful behaviour this week.

Personal Growth Reflection:

- Where did I practise staying powerful this week?

- What challenged me about leading myself and managing my responses?
- How did staying powerful impact my relationships or our staff culture?
- Where do I want to keep growing next week?

WEEK 13:

CHOOSING LOVE OVER FEAR IN STAFF RELATIONSHIPS

"In a culture of love, we choose connection over control,
love over fear, and people over problems."

Discuss:

- What does choosing love over fear look like in our staff relationships?
- Where does fear show up in school culture?
- What happens when we respond with love instead of fear?

Learn:

Fear disconnects us. It causes us to react, control, avoid, or shut down. In staff culture, fear shows up as gossip, assumptions, defensiveness, or withholding trust.

Love draws us closer. It builds connection, courage, and safety. Love says: "I care enough to stay connected even when it's hard."

We can choose love over fear by:

- Staying curious instead of making assumptions
- Listening well before responding
- Speaking the truth with kindness
- Creating safety in conflict
- Valuing people more than problems

Love creates space for growth and restoration. Fear isolates, divides, and controls.

Demonstrate:

Tissue vs Rope Relationships

Bring a piece of tissue paper and a length of rope.

Explain:

- Tissue relationships are fragile—built on fear, control, avoidance, or disconnection. They can't hold weight or withstand pressure. One pull and they tear.
- Rope relationships are strong—built on love, trust, respect, and clear communication. They can hold tension, handle mistakes, and withstand pressure because both people hold their end with responsibility.

Discuss:

- What kind of relationships are we building in our staff culture?
- Are we responding with love (building rope relationships) or fear (creating tissue-thin connections)?
- How can we each strengthen our relational "rope" this week?

Leader Share:

As the host of this session, share a story of when you noticed the difference between responding from fear (disconnection) versus responding from love (connection) in your leadership. What was the outcome?

Our School Statement:

Together, write your school statement for the week.

For example: *"In this school, we choose love over fear in every relationship."*

In this school,

Connect Groups:

- Share a time when choosing love over fear changed a situation.
- Where does fear show up in staff culture, and how can we respond differently?
- How can we practise choosing love this week?

My Goal This Week:

Write one small, specific action you can take to practise choosing love over fear this week.

Personal Growth Reflection:

- Where did I practise choosing connection (love) over discon-nection (fear) this week?
- What challenged me about staying connected?
- How did love impact my relationships or staff culture?
- Where do I want to keep growing next week?

WEEK 14:

BOUNDARIES THAT CREATE FREEDOM AND CLARITY

"In a culture of love, boundaries protect what matters most and create clarity for healthy connection."

Discuss:

- What are healthy boundaries in a staff culture?
- How do boundaries create both freedom and clarity?
- What happens when boundaries are unclear or ignored?

Learn:

Boundaries are not walls to keep people out—they are fences that clearly mark what we are responsible for and what we are not. Healthy boundaries protect our energy, our time, our well-being, and our relationships.

In a staff culture, clear boundaries:

- Communicate expectations
- Build trust
- Prevent burnout
- Clarify responsibilities
- Support respect for one another

Boundaries create freedom because everyone knows what is okay, what isn't okay, and what belongs to them to manage.

Unclear boundaries lead to frustration, conflict, overcommitment, and disconnection.

Demonstrate:

You will need a Nerf gun and the boundary circles from Week 9–– these will become your targets for this activity.

Ask a series of scenario-based questions. Invite one volunteer staff member to shoot a nerf gun towards the target in response to each scenario. Mark where their shot lands and asked if this is what they believe.

Example Questions:

- Managing my own emotions when I feel stressed.
- Taking responsibility for another staff member's workload.
- Preparing for my own lessons or duties.
- Fixing someone else's mistake without a conversation.
- Setting healthy boundaries for work-life balance.

- Controlling how a student responds in every situation.
- Seeking feedback to improve my own practice.

The lesson is that we need to be intentional about knowing our boundaries and aiming with focus—not just shooting aimlessly.

Reflect together:

- What happens when we aren't intentional about our boundaries?
- How does this demonstration remind us that healthy boundaries require clarity and intentional focus?

Boundaries are not about controlling others—they are about being clear and intentional about what belongs to us to manage and protect.

Leader Share:

As the host of this session, share a story of when clear boundaries helped you lead well or prevented burnout. Or, share a time when unclear boundaries created frustration and what you learned.

Our School Statement:

Together, write your school statement for the week.

For example: *"In this school, we set clear boundaries that protect what matters most."*

In this school,

Connect Groups:

- Share a time when boundaries helped you in your role.

- Where do we need clearer boundaries in our staff culture?

- How can we practise setting or respecting boundaries this week?

My Goal This Week:

Write one small, specific action you can take to practise healthy boundaries this week.

Personal Growth Reflection:

- Where did I practise setting or respecting boundaries well this week?

- What challenged me about boundaries?

- How did boundaries impact my well-being or relationships?

- Where do I want to keep growing next week?

WEEK 15:

RESPECT AND CONNECT ACROSS DIVERSE TEAMS

"In a culture of love, respect means valuing every person, every role, and every story."

Discuss:

- What does respect look like in a diverse staff team?
- How do we connect well with people who are different to us?
- What happens when respect is missing in a team?

Learn:

Every staff team is made up of diverse people—different backgrounds, experiences, roles, strengths, and personalities. Respect means choosing to value people because they are human, not because they are the same as us.

Healthy connection happens when we:

- Listen without judgement
- Show curiosity rather than assumption
- Honour different perspectives
- Collaborate across roles
- Speak with kindness even when we disagree

Respect creates connection. Disrespect creates distance.

Demonstrate:

Bring a puzzle (a children's puzzle is preferable). Hand out the puzzle pieces to different staff and then have them work on the puzzle together. Show how each piece (and person) is unique, but every piece is needed to create the whole picture.

Reflect together:

- What happens when we try to make every piece the same?
- How does diversity strengthen our team?

Leader Share:

As the host of this session, share a story of when respecting differences helped build a stronger relationship or team culture. Or share a time when misunderstanding or disrespect created distance and what you learned.

Our School Statement:

Together, write your school statement for the week.

For example: *"In this school, we respect every person and build connection across our differences."*

In this school,

Connect Groups:

- Share a time when respecting differences strengthened a relationship.
- Where can we practise better respect and connection in our staff team?
- How can we honour diversity and build connection this week?

My Goal This Week:

Write one small, specific action you can take to practise respect and connection well this week.

Personal Growth Reflection:

- Where did I practise respect and connection well this week?
- What challenged me about connecting across differences?
- How did respect impact our staff culture?
- Where do I want to keep growing next week?

WEEK 16:

GROWING AND TAKING RESPONSIBILITY FOR CULTURE

"In a culture of love, every person plays a part in creating and protecting a healthy workplace culture."

Discuss:

- What does taking responsibility for our school culture look like?
- How do we each contribute to a positive or negative culture?
- What happens when people wait for someone else to lead culture change?

Learn:

Culture is not created by accident—it is shaped every day by what we celebrate, tolerate, and role-model. Healthy school culture happens when every staff member chooses to lead themselves well and contribute to a positive environment.

Taking responsibility for culture means:

- Living out the values we say we believe
- Modelling respect, kindness, and honesty
- Owning mistakes and learning from them
- Speaking up when things aren't right
- Encouraging and building others up

Culture grows when people take responsibility for their impact and influence.

Demonstrate:

Create a "culture garden" visual with paper flowers or plants. Each staff member writes one positive action or attitude that helps grow a healthy culture. Display the garden in the staffroom or workspace as a reminder that culture needs daily tending.

Leader Share:

As the host of this session, share a story of when you saw positive culture growth because someone took responsibility and led by example. Or share a lesson you learned about how culture is impacted by small daily choices.

Our School Statement:

Together, write your school statement for the week.

For example: *"In this school, we each take responsibility for creating a culture of respect, care, and connection."*

In this school,

Connect Groups:

- Share a time when you saw culture improve because of staff ownership.
- What are small actions we can each take to grow a healthy culture?
- How can we practise taking responsibility for culture this week?

My Goal This Week:

Write one small, specific action you can take to practise taking responsibility for culture this week.

Personal Growth Reflection:

- Where did I practise taking responsibility for culture this week?
- What challenged me about contributing to culture?
- How did my actions impact our staff environment?
- Where do I want to keep growing next week?

WEEK 17:

LEARNING FROM MISTAKES WITH LOVE AND HUMILITY

"In a culture of love, mistakes are seen as opportunities for learning, growth, and restoration."

Discuss:

- How does our staff culture currently respond to mistakes?
- What makes it hard to own mistakes?
- How does love and humility change the way we respond to errors?

Learn:

Mistakes are inevitable—in our students, in our leadership, and in ourselves. The goal is not perfection; the goal is learning and growth.

A culture of love responds to mistakes with humility, curiosity, and courage.

When mistakes happen, powerful people:

- Own their part without excuses
- Apologise sincerely if needed
- Learn from the experience
- Repair and restore connection
- Grow through reflection

Love removes shame from mistakes. Humility keeps us teachable.

Demonstrate:

Use a crumpled bank note or a jar of broken crayons. Discuss:

- Are these items ruined? Or can they still be useful?
- How does this remind us that mistakes do not define our value?

Mistakes do not disqualify us—they invite us to grow.

Leader Share:

As the host of this session, share a story of when you learned from a mistake in leadership. What did you do to repair the situation? What did you learn about love, humility, or responsibility?

Our School Statement:

Together, write your school statement for the week.

For example: *"In this school, we learn from mistakes with love, humility, and responsibility."*

In this school,

Connect Groups:

- Share a time when learning from a mistake helped you grow.
- How can we create a safe culture for mistakes and learning?
- How can we practise love and humility this week?

My Goal This Week:

Write one small, specific action you can take to practise learning from mistakes well this week.

Personal Growth Reflection:

- Where did I practise love and humility in response to mistakes this week?
- What challenged me about owning mistakes?
- How did this impact our staff relationships or culture?
- Where do I want to keep growing next week?

WEEK 18:

HELPING EACH OTHER GROW PERSONALLY AND PROFESSIONALLY

"In a culture of love, growth happens best in community— where we encourage, challenge, and support one another."

Discuss:

- What helps us grow personally and professionally in our staff culture?
- What happens when we support each other's growth?
- What gets in the way of encouraging others?

Learn:

We grow best when we don't grow alone. Healthy teams create a culture of encouragement, feedback, and support. Growth is not just about skills or knowledge—it's about becoming better people who contribute positively to the whole community.

Helping others grow means:

- Offering encouragement
- Giving constructive feedback
- Sharing resources and ideas
- Celebrating progress
- Creating space for mistakes and learning

When we lift others, we lift the whole team.

Demonstrate:

Give each staff member a stack of sticky notes. Invite them to write how they have seen each person in the room grow—personally or professionally. Stick the notes on each other's backs without saying what was written. Don't remove the sticky notes until you get to your connect groups.

Leader Share:

As the host of this session, share a story of when someone helped you grow professionally or personally. What did they do that made a difference? How has that shaped the way you help others?

Our School Statement:

Together, write your school statement for the week.

For example: *"In this school, we help each other grow through encouragement, feedback, and support."*

In this school,

Connect Groups:
Invite each person to read their notes silently and reflect together:

- What did you notice about how others see your growth?
- How does it feel to have your growth recognised?
- How can we help each other grow in our staff culture?

My Goal This Week:
Write one small, specific action you can take to help someone else grow this week.

Personal Growth Reflection:
- Where did I practise helping others grow this week?
- What challenged me about encouraging or supporting others?
- How did this impact our staff culture?
- Where do I want to keep growing next week?

WEEK 19:

STICKING WITH IT—CONSISTENCY IN CHALLENGING TIMES

"In a culture of love, consistency builds trust, creates safety, and sustains culture even when things are hard."

Discuss:

- Why is consistency important in our staff culture?
- What makes it hard to stay consistent when things are challenging?
- What impact does consistency have on students and staff?

Learn:

Consistency is doing what we say we will do—again and again. It means showing up with integrity even when it's difficult or inconvenient. In school culture, consistency builds safety because people know what to expect.

Consistency looks like:

- Following through on commitments
- Holding boundaries kindly but firmly
- Leading ourselves well under pressure
- Staying calm and present
- Modelling our values regardless of circumstances

Consistency is not perfection—it's about staying committed to what matters most over time.

Demonstrate:

Bring a jar of small stones or marbles. Each stone represents a consistent action or behaviour. Slowly add them to a clear jar. Reflect together:

- How do small actions build trust over time?
- What happens when consistency breaks down?

Trust grows one action at a time.

Leader Share:

As the host of this session, share a story of when consistency helped build trust or a positive culture, especially during a challenging season. What did you learn about staying committed to your values?

Our School Statement:

Together, write your school statement for the week.

For example: *"In this school, we practise consistency to build trust and create safety for everyone."*

In this school,

Connect Groups:

- Share a time when consistency built trust in your role or relationships.
- What is one area where you want to grow in consistency?
- How can we support each other to stay consistent this week?

My Goal This Week:

Write one small, specific action you can take to practise consistency this week.

Personal Growth Reflection:

- Where did I practise consistency well this week?
- What challenged me about staying consistent?
- How did consistency impact our staff culture or relationships?
- Where do I want to keep growing next week?

WEEK 20:

JOYFUL RESPONSIBILITY—OWNING OUR ROLE IN CULTURE

"In a culture of love, responsibility is not a burden—it's a privilege that brings joy, purpose, and growth."

Discuss:

- What does joyful responsibility look like in our staff culture?
- What helps us take responsibility with joy rather than pressure?
- How does personal ownership shape a healthy team?

Learn:

Responsibility is not just about getting tasks done—it's about owning our role in creating a positive, thriving workplace culture. Joyful responsibility means we approach our work with purpose, enthusiasm, and a willingness to grow.

Joyful responsibility looks like:

- Owning my attitude and effort
- Taking pride in my role
- Supporting others without taking over
- Responding to challenges with curiosity, not defensiveness
- Bringing positive energy and encouragement

When we each own our role with joy, we create a staff culture that is resilient, hopeful, and connected.

Demonstrate:

Bring a basket of different tools (e.g., pen, scissors, tape, markers). Each represents a unique role or contribution in the school. Reflect together:

- What happens when a tool doesn't do its job?
- What happens when we all own our part with joy?

Healthy culture happens when every role is valued and fulfilled with care.

Leader Share:

As the host of this session, share a story of when taking joyful responsibility changed your perspective or helped strengthen your team. What did you learn about ownership and contribution?

Our School Statement:

Together, write your school statement for the week.

For example: *"In this school, we take joyful responsibility for creating a positive culture together."*

In this school,

Connect Groups:

- Share a time when joyful responsibility made a difference in your role.
- What helps you bring joy and purpose to your work?
- How can we practise joyful responsibility together this week?

My Goal This Week:

Write one small, specific action you can take to practise joyful responsibility this week.

Personal Growth Reflection:

- Where did I practise joyful responsibility well this week?
- What challenged me about taking ownership?
- How did joyful responsibility impact our staff culture?
- Where do I want to keep growing next week?

PART THREE

ACHIEVING GENUINE RESTORATION IN OUR WORKPLACE RELATIONSHIPS

Restoration brings strength, not weakness.

Every school has moments of tension, conflict, or disconnection. It's part of working in a fast-paced, emotionally demanding environment. What defines a strong staff culture is not avoiding these moments, but how we respond to them when they happen.

This section focuses on the heart of genuine restoration: the willingness to repair, not just move on. It's about acknowledging when something's gone wrong, listening without defensiveness, and choosing to rebuild trust with honesty and care.

In staff culture, restoration can look like clearing up a miscommunication, making space for someone's perspective, offering a sincere apology, or choosing grace over blame. These actions aren't signs of weakness—they are signs of emotional maturity and shared commitment.

When we practise restoration well, we create a workplace where people feel safe to be human—to grow, to try again, and to keep showing up for each other. That's the kind of culture students notice. That's the kind of culture that lasts.

WEEK 21:

THE ART OF APOLOGY IN PROFESSIONAL RELATIONSHIPS

"In a culture of love, an apology is not about blame or shame—it's about ownership, restoration, and reconnection."

Discuss:

- What makes a genuine apology?
- Why is it sometimes difficult to apologise in professional settings?
- How does a healthy apology strengthen trust and connection?

Learn:

The art of apology is a powerful tool for repairing relationships and protecting workplace culture. A genuine apology is not about fixing everything instantly but about taking ownership of our actions and their impact on others.

A healthy apology includes:

- Recognising the impact of our actions
- Avoiding excuses or blame
- Taking full responsibility
- Expressing sincere regret
- Asking what is needed for restoration

An apology is a bridge back to connection.

Demonstrate:

Bring a rope to represent relationships. When a mess is made and disconnection enters a relationship it's like the rope has been dropped (drop one side). Explain that the rope can be used in two ways: as a tool for safety and connection (we can apologise), or misused as a whip that causes further hurt when trust is already fragile.

Talk through the steps of a healthy apology—ownership, apology, consistent action—demonstrating how holding the rope with care helps restore connection and build trust again.

Discuss together:

- What happens when we misuse the "rope" in our relationships?
- How does this demonstration remind us that restoring connection requires intentionality, safety, and responsibility?

Healthy relationships use the rope to build safety, not to control or hurt.

- What happens when we expect connection to return instantly?
- How does this demonstration remind us that restoration is a process?

Genuine apologies repair connection because they communicate value and respect.

Leader Share:

As the host of this session, share a story of a time when an apology helped restore a relationship in your professional life. What did you learn about humility, courage, or connection?

Our School Statement:

Together, write your school statement for the week.

For example: *"In this school, we practise the art of apology to restore trust and connection."*

In this school,

Connect Groups:

- Share a time when an apology restored trust in a relationship.
- What helps us apologise well in our staff culture?
- How can we model healthy apologies this week?

My Goal This Week:

Write one small, specific action you can take to practise the art of apology this week.

Personal Growth Reflection:

- Where did I practise healthy apology well this week?
- What challenged me about taking ownership or apologising?
- How did apology impact our staff culture or relationships?
- Where do I want to keep growing next week?

WEEK 22:

FORGIVENESS AND MOVING FORWARD AS A TEAM

"In a culture of love, forgiveness is a choice to let go of offence so we can move forward with freedom and connection."

Discuss:

- What does forgiveness look like in a staff culture?
- Why is forgiveness important in professional relationships?
- What happens when we hold onto offence?

Learn:

Forgiveness is not about forgetting or excusing poor behaviour—it's about releasing ourselves from the weight of offence. In a healthy staff culture, forgiveness clears the path for restoration, teamwork, and trust to be rebuilt.

Forgiveness looks like:

- Choosing to release bitterness and resentment
- Separating the action from the person's value
- Creating space for restoration and growth
- Letting go so we can move forward freely

Forgiveness does not mean there are no boundaries—it means we refuse to stay stuck in hurt or anger.

Demonstrate:

Place a mousetrap on the table. Point out that the cheese (or other food item) is like an "Offence."

Explain that offence often looks tempting to hold onto—we feel justified, angry, or protective. But just like a mouse nibbling at the bait, when we nibble on the offence, we end up hurting ourselves more than anyone else.

Demonstrate by using a prop (like a small toy mouse or stick with a paper mouse attached) to show the mouse taking the bait and getting snapped in the trap.

Discuss together:

- What happens when we hold onto offence?
- How does this demonstration remind us of the cost of unforgiveness?

Forgiveness frees us from the trap of offence so we can move forward in freedom and connection.

Leader Share:

As the host of this session, share a story of when forgiveness allowed you to move forward in a professional relationship. What was the impact on you and the culture of your team?

Our School Statement:

Together, write your school statement for the week.

For example: *"In this school, we choose forgiveness to create freedom and connection."*

In this school,

Connect Groups:

- Share a time when forgiveness helped restore a relationship.
- What helps you forgive in a staff culture?
- How can we practise forgiveness together this week?

My Goal This Week:

Write one small, specific action you can take to practise forgiveness this week.

Personal Growth Reflection:

- Where did I practise forgiveness well this week?
- What challenged me about letting go of offence?
- How did forgiveness impact our staff culture or relationships?
- Where do I want to keep growing next week?

WEEK 23:

RESTORING TRUST AFTER MISTAKES OR CONFLICT

"In a culture of love, trust is rebuilt through honesty, humility, and consistent action over time."

Discuss:

- Why is restoring trust important in staff relationships?
- What helps rebuild trust after mistakes or conflict?
- What happens if we avoid doing the work of restoration?

Learn:

Trust can be damaged quickly but is always rebuilt slowly. In professional relationships, restoring trust takes time, courage, and consistent actions that prove we are safe, reliable, and respectful.

Restoring trust looks like:

- Owning our mistakes without excuses
- Apologising sincerely
- Listening without defensiveness
- Following through on commitments
- Showing consistency over time

Trust is restored when people feel safe again—not just when words are spoken, but when actions align with those words.

Demonstrate:

Bring two glass jars. Fill one jar with clear, clean water labelled "Trust."' In the other jar, add a few drops of food colouring to represent "Mistakes or Conflict."

Slowly and carefully, pour clean water back into the coloured jar to show that restoring trust takes time, patience, and consistent effort to dilute the impact of mistakes and rebuild clarity.

Discuss together:

- What happens when we expect trust to return instantly?
- How does this demonstration remind us that restoration is a process?

Leader Share:

As the host of this session, share a story of when you needed to rebuild trust with someone in your professional life. What steps did you take? What did you learn about restoration?

Our School Statement:

Together, write your school statement for the week.

For example: *"In this school, we restore trust through honesty, humility, and consistent action."*

In this school,

Connect Groups:

- Share a time when trust was restored in a relationship.
- What small actions rebuild trust over time?
- How can we practise restoring trust this week?

My Goal This Week:

Write one small, specific action you can take to practise rebuilding trust this week.

Personal Growth Reflection:

- Where did I practise restoring trust well this week?
- What challenged me about rebuilding trust?
- How did trust restoration impact our staff culture or relationships?
- Where do I want to keep growing next week?

WEEK 24:

SECOND CHANCES AND AN UMBRELLA OF GRACE

*"In a culture of love, second chances create space
for growth, learning, and restoration."*

Discuss:

- Why are second chances important in staff and student relationships?

- What happens when we don't offer grace for mistakes?

- How does creating a safe space help people grow?

Learn:

We all need second chances. Mistakes are part of learning, and grace allows people to try again without fear of shame or punishment. In professional relationships, offering second chances nurtures trust, courage, and personal growth.

Second chances look like:

- Creating safe spaces for honest conversation
- Responding with empathy and care
- Communicating clear expectations for growth
- Valuing progress over perfection

Grace doesn't mean avoiding accountability—it means holding both truth and kindness.

Demonstrate:

Bring an umbrella and attach a sign that says "Grace." Explain that the umbrella represents a safe place for people to come when they need to talk about mistakes, seek understanding, or ask for a second chance.

Provide these examples:

Student Example (Playground): A student reacts unkindly during a game. Instead of sending them away immediately, invite them to step under the "umbrella of grace" and talk through what happened and how they could clean up their mess.

Staff Example: A colleague is on their phone or device during a meeting. Instead of responding with frustration, you offer them a conversation under the 'umbrella of grace' to understand, clarify expectations, and move forward with connection.

Invite staff to imagine scenarios where students or colleagues might need to step under the "umbrella of grace." Role-model how this conversation might look and sound in your school culture.

Discuss together:

- How can offering grace change the outcome of difficult situations?
- What happens when people know they are safe to be honest?
- How do we create an "umbrella of grace" in our staff culture?

Leader Share:

As the host of this session, share a story of when someone offered you a second chance or extended grace that helped you grow. What impact did it have on your professional relationships or leadership?

Our School Statement:

Together, write your school statement for the week.

For example: *"In this school, we offer second chances and create safe spaces of grace for learning and growth."*

In this school,

Connect Groups:

- Share a time when you received a second chance and how it helped you grow.
- How can we offer grace and second chances in our staff culture?
- What does creating a safe space for mistakes look like this week?

My Goal This Week:

Write one small, specific action you can take to practise offering grace or second chances this week.

Personal Growth Reflection:

- What challenged me about creating space for mistakes?
- What happened when I put up an umbrella of grace for myself or someone else this week?
- How did second chances impact our staff culture or relationships?
- Where do I want to keep growing next week?

WEEK 25:

TAKING RESPONSIBILITY IN PROFESSIONAL RELATIONSHIPS

"In a culture of love, taking responsibility builds trust, respect, and personal integrity."

Discuss:

- What does taking responsibility look like in a staff culture?
- What happens when we avoid responsibility or shift blame?
- How does responsibility strengthen trust and connection?

Learn:

Healthy teams are built on people who lead themselves well. Taking responsibility means owning our actions, words, and attitude—regardless of what others are doing. It means saying, "I choose to manage myself well and do what I can to repair or improve this situation."

Responsibility looks like:

- Owning my part in mistakes or misunderstandings
- Communicating clearly and respectfully
- Taking initiative to problem-solve
- Following through on commitments
- Responding with integrity, even in hard moments

Responsibility invites connection because it shows we can be trusted.

Demonstrate:

Bring a lamp with a bendy neck. Explain that taking responsibility is like pointing the light at ourselves—shining a spotlight on what belongs to us to manage: our choices, our words, our attitude.

Every time we choose to blame someone else, it's like turning the light away from ourselves and shining it on them instead—avoiding responsibility and focusing on their actions instead of our own.

Demonstrate this by physically moving the lamp to shine on yourself when taking ownership, and turning it away to shine on someone else when shifting blame.

Discuss together:

- What happens when we keep the light on ourselves?
- How does this demonstration remind us that taking responsibility keeps us growing and connected?

Leader Share:

As the host of this session, share a story of a time when taking responsibility helped you repair a situation or strengthen a relationship. What did you learn?

Our School Statement:

Together, write your school statement for the week.

For example: *"In this school, we take responsibility for our words, actions, and relationships."*

In this school,

Connect Groups:

- Share a time when taking responsibility helped a situation improve.
- What does personal responsibility look like in our staff culture?
- How can we practise taking responsibility this week?

My Goal This Week:

Write one small, specific action you can take to practise taking responsibility this week.

Personal Growth Reflection:

- Where did I practise taking responsibility well this week?
- What challenged me about owning my part?

- How did taking responsibility impact our staff culture or relationships?
- Where do I want to keep growing next week?

WEEK 26:

POWERFUL FRIENDSHIPS THAT STRENGTHEN STAFF TEAMS

"In a culture of love, powerful friendships are built on trust, honesty, and respect—not control or dependence."

Discuss:

- What do you believe friendships should look like at work? Notice how everyone will have a different answer. Some people like to keep work and personal life separate, while others enjoy spending lots of time with their colleagues outside of work. Both are valid.

- What makes a friendship powerful in a staff culture?

- What happens when workplace friendships become controlling or exclusive?

- How can we build healthy connection while maintaining personal responsibility?

Learn:

Powerful friendships are relationships where both people lead themselves well and create space for each other to thrive. They aren't built on control, gossip, or dependence, but on respect, honesty, and support.

Powerful friendships look like:

- Encouraging each other to grow
- Speaking honestly with kindness
- Holding healthy boundaries
- Supporting without rescuing or controlling
- Celebrating each other's wins

Powerful friendships strengthen a whole team because they model respect, connection, and personal responsibility.

Demonstrate:

Use a table or small desk to illustrate the idea of connection and responsibility in powerful friendships.

Invite two staff members to each hold one side of the table (remind them to use proper lifting techniques––otherwise imagine, don't lift) . Explain that strong friendships require both people to stay connected and hold their side with respect and responsibility.

Demonstrate how, if one person lets go or steps away, the table becomes unstable and can't be carried or moved well. Likewise, if one person tries to drag the table without the other person's cooperation, the relationship is strained or damaged.

Discuss together:

- What happens when one person isn't holding their side of the friendship?
- How does this demonstration remind us that powerful friendships require effort, respect, and shared responsibility from both people?

Leader Share:

As the host of this session, share a story of a workplace friendship that strengthened your leadership or character. What made that friendship powerful?

Our School Statement:

Together, write your school statement for the week.

For example: *"In this school, we build powerful friendships through respect, honesty, and shared responsibility."*

In this school,

Connect Groups:

- Share a time when a powerful friendship helped you grow.
- What does respect and responsibility look like in workplace friendships?
- How can we build powerful friendships this week?

My Goal This Week:

Write one small, specific action you can take to practise building powerful friendships this week.

Personal Growth Reflection:

- Where did I practise building powerful friendships well this week?

- What challenged me about maintaining respect and responsibility?

- How did powerful friendships impact our staff culture or relationships?

- Where do I want to keep growing next week?

WEEK 27:

BECOMING A POWERFUL PERSON IN EVERY SPACE

"In a culture of love, powerful people take responsibility for themselves, bring safety to others, and lead with respect no matter where they are."

Discuss:

- What does it mean to be a powerful person at work?
- What happens when we give away our power by blaming, avoiding, or controlling others?
- What are some qualities of powerful people you admire?

Learn:

Being powerful doesn't mean being the loudest or most in control. It means managing yourself well no matter where you are or who you're with. Powerful people bring safety, clarity, and respect into every space they enter.

Powerful people:

- Manage their emotions
- Take responsibility for their words and actions
- Respect boundaries
- Speak honestly with kindness
- Stay calm in conflict
- Respond rather than react

Being a powerful person means you don't need to control others because you can control yourself.

Demonstrate:

Remind staff of the three aspects of being a powerful person from earlier in the series:

1. Requiring respectful relationships.
2. Setting limits and boundaries because they value themselves.
3. Managing themselves regardless of what others are doing.

Ask staff to take a moment to reflect on these three qualities and rate themselves out of 10 for each area:

- How well have I practised requiring respectful relationships?
- How well have I set healthy limits and boundaries?
- How well have I managed myself regardless of others?

Once they have given themselves a score, share with the person next to them:

- What would help me move just +1 point higher in each area?
- What small action could I take this week to lead myself even better?

Leader Share:

As the host of this session, share a story of a time when you chose to be a powerful person in a difficult situation. What helped you respond well? What was the impact on others?

Our School Statement:

Together, write your school statement for the week.

For example: *"In this school, we choose to be powerful people who bring joy, responsibility and connection into every space."*

In this school,

Connect Groups:

- Share a time when you felt powerful (respect, boundaries, self-control) in a situation.
- What helps you stay powerful in challenging spaces?
- How can we practise being powerful people in our school this week?

My Goal This Week:

Write one small, specific action you can take to practise being a powerful person this week.

Personal Growth Reflection:

- Where did I practise being a powerful person well this week?
- What challenged me about leading myself well?
- How did choosing to stay powerful impact my staff culture or relationships?
- Where do I want to keep growing next week?

WEEK 28:

RESTORING SELF-RESPECT AND PROFESSIONAL CONFIDENCE

"In a culture of love, we treat ourselves with the same value, care, and responsibility we extend to others."

Discuss:

- What does self-respect look like in our professional lives?
- How do we rebuild confidence after a difficult moment or season?
- What happens when we forget to honour our own value?

Learn:

Self-respect is the foundation of professional confidence. It's about remembering your worth—not because of your performance, but because of who you are. In a busy and demanding school environment, it's easy to forget this, especially after mistakes, failures, or burnout.

When we restore self-respect, we:

- Speak to ourselves with kindness, not criticism
- Set healthy expectations and boundaries
- Remember our "why" and reconnect with our purpose
- Take pride in our progress, not just perfection

Confidence grows when we choose self-respect, especially in hard seasons. In doing so, we create a culture where others feel safe to value themselves too.

Demonstrate:

Bring a small mirror and a permanent marker. Ask, "What kinds of things do we sometimes say to ourselves after a mistake?" As staff offer responses (e.g. "I'm not good enough," "I've failed again"), write these on the mirror.

Then, slowly wipe them away using glass cleaner and a cloth, revealing the clear reflection again. Share:

"These thoughts might stick for a while, but they're not who we are. Self-respect is choosing to see clearly again and speak to ourselves with truth and kindness."

Leader Share:

As the host, share a time when you lost confidence in your role—maybe after a failure, a conflict, or a tough term—and how you rebuilt it by choosing self-respect. What helped you restore your confidence without relying on external approval?

Our School Statement:

Together, write your school statement for the week.

For example: *"In this school, we treat ourselves with the same respect we offer others."*

In this school,

Connect Groups:

- Share a time when you struggled with confidence. What helped you get back up?
- What does healthy self-respect look like for you right now?
- How can we encourage self-respect and confidence in our team this week?

My Goal This Week:

Write one small, specific action you can take to restore or protect your self-respect this week.

Personal Growth Journal:

- Where did I practise self-respect this week?
- What challenged me about rebuilding confidence?
- How did self-respect impact my mindset or relationships?
- Where do I want to keep growing next week?

WEEK 29:

TAKING INITIATIVE WITH THE EMPOWERMENT MODEL

"In a culture of love, we take ownership for what we see and step up with empathy, courage, and care."

Discuss:

- What does healthy initiative look like in a staff culture?
- What's the difference between helping and taking over?
- What happens when we wait for others to step up?

Learn:

Initiative is a hallmark of powerful people. It means noticing a need and choosing to respond—not by rescuing or controlling, but by stepping in with responsibility and wisdom. In strong teams, initiative is not just appreciated, it's expected.

The Empowerment Model helps us do this well. It gives us a framework to support others while still taking ownership of what's ours to do.

The Empowerment Model includes:

1. **Empathy**: I take time to understand.
2. **Empower**: I believe in others' ability to grow.
3. **Explore**: I ask questions and stay curious.
4. **Educate**: I share insights without shame.
5. **Expect**: I set clear, healthy expectations.
6. **Encourage**: I celebrate growth and progress.

When we take initiative using this model, we help others rise without stepping on their toes.

Demonstrate:

Place a stack of random objects on a tray (e.g. a cup, a book, a stapler, some scrunched-up paper). Invite a volunteer to carry the tray across the room—but don't tell them it's unbalanced. Midway across the room, an item will likely fall.

When it does, pause the activity and invite others to step in and help—but set a twist:

One person is allowed to help only if they ask permission first, one is allowed to offer suggestions but not touch, and one can take over completely without asking.

Reflect together:

- Which approach helped most?

- How did each action feel from the perspective of the person carrying the tray?
- What does this reveal about initiative, support, and boundaries?

True initiative includes empathy, permission, and partnership. The Empowerment Model keeps us helpful *without becoming overpowering.*

Leader Share:

As the host of this session, share a time when someone took initiative in your school community in a way that helped others grow—not just fix the problem. What made it empowering? What can we learn from their approach?

Our School Statement:

Together, write your school statement for the week.

For example: *"In this school, we take initiative with empathy and responsibility, not control."*

In this school,

Connect Groups:

- Share a time when you saw initiative done well. What made it respectful and effective?
- Where do you see a need this week where you could step up and help?
- How can we use the Empowerment Model to take initiative in a way that builds others?

My Goal This Week:

Write one small, specific action you can take to practise healthy initiative this week.

Personal Growth Reflection:

- Where did I take initiative well this week?

- What challenged me about stepping in or stepping back?

- How did my actions impact our staff relationships or culture?

- Where do I want to keep growing next week?

WEEK 30:

BEING A ROLE MODEL IN STAFF CULTURE

"In a culture of love, we model the kind of people and professionals we hope others will become."

Discuss:

- What does being a role model mean to you?
- Who has been a positive role model in your professional life? What made them stand out?
- How do our everyday actions influence others—even when we don't realise it?

Learn:

In every school, culture is being shaped—not just by big policies or meetings, but by the small daily choices made by each team member. Role-modelling isn't about being perfect. It's about being intentional.

Being a role model means we:

- Stay calm when others are reactive
- Speak with kindness even in pressure
- Take responsibility without shifting blame
- Own our boundaries and respect others'
- Show humility, courage, and growth

Whether we notice it or not, others are learning from how we respond, lead, speak, and show up. Our example speaks louder than our advice.

Demonstrate:

Bring in a piece of tracing paper, a bold black marker, and a soft pencil. Use the marker to write a short word on a plain sheet underneath (e.g. "respect" or "growth").

Place the tracing paper over the top and invite a volunteer to trace over the word using the pencil. Then, give another person a second tracing paper, but this time distort the base word—make it messy, faded, or scribbled over. Ask them to trace it again.

Compare the two tracings. Ask:

- What made it easier to follow one than the other?
- How does this relate to what we model for others in our team or classroom?

What we model—clearly or unclearly, intentionally or accidentally—leaves a pattern for others to follow. When we're consistent and clear, we help shape the path.

Leader Share:

As the host of this session, share a story of someone who modelled something that shaped your practice or leadership. How did their example stay with you? Or share a time you realised others were following your example—for better or for worse.

Our School Statement:

Together, write your school statement for the week.

For example: *"In this school, we lead by example, not just intention."*

In this school,

Connect Groups:

- Share a time when someone's example helped you grow.
- What do you think you are modelling most often in your role—both intentionally and unintentionally?
- What's one area you want to model more intentionally this week?

My Goal This Week:

Write one small, specific action you can take to be a more intentional role model this week.

Personal Growth Reflection:

- Where did I model healthy staff culture this week?

- What challenged me about leading by example?
- How did my example impact others?
- Where do I want to keep growing next week?

PART FOUR

EMPOWERING LEADERSHIP
AT EVERY LEVEL

Leadership is something we practise, not just a role we hold.

In every school, leadership isn't just found in the principal's office. It's found in the way we speak to each other, respond to challenges, and support those around us. Whether we're leading a classroom, a team, a conversation, or simply ourselves, leadership is woven into everyday moments.

This section invites staff to reimagine leadership as something that lives in all of us—not based on position, but on influence, character, and courage. It's about taking initiative, modelling connection, and being someone others can rely on.

Empowered leadership doesn't mean doing everything. It means showing up with intention, lifting others, and using our words and actions to build trust and clarity. It's how we create momentum in our school culture—one person at a time.

When leadership is shared, the whole team grows. Students benefit. Staff feel trusted. And the culture becomes something we're all proud to carry forward together.

WEEK 31:

SERVICE TO OTHERS—LEADING WITH PURPOSE

"In a culture of love, leadership is not about position—it's about choosing to serve with intention and heart."

Discuss:

- What does leadership through service look like in a school setting?
- How does serving others help build trust and connection?
- What's the difference between helping from a place of obligation versus a place of purpose?

Learn:

Leadership is not a title—it's a choice we make every day to show up, support others, and take responsibility for what we bring into a space.

When we lead with purpose, we're not just completing tasks—we're contributing to culture.

Service-based leadership looks like:

- Stepping in without needing credit
- Offering support without controlling
- Seeing and valuing what others need
- Encouraging growth in others while leading ourselves well
- Creating space where others feel seen, safe, and strengthened

True service isn't about doing more—it's about being present and intentional in what you do.

Demonstrate:

Place a selection of shoes in the middle of the group (you can use real ones or cutouts/pictures): sports shoes, work boots, high heels, slippers, school shoes. Ask each person to choose a shoe that represents a kind of leadership or service they've seen or offered.

Invite a few people to share:

- Why did you choose that shoe?
- How does it represent the way you serve others or lead?

Service doesn't look the same for everyone. The key is not what shoes you wear—it's that you choose to walk with purpose and help others along the way.

Leader Share:

As the host of this session, share a story of someone who served quietly and consistently—someone whose leadership came through care, presence, or behind-the-scenes support. What made their leadership so impactful?

Our School Statement:

Together, write your school statement for the week.

For example: *"In this school, we lead by serving others with purpose and care."*

In this school,

Connect Groups:

- Share a time when someone's act of service inspired you.
- What kind of service or support do you find most meaningful to receive?
- How can we serve each other intentionally this week?

My Goal This Week:

Write one small, specific action you can take to lead through service this week.

Personal Growth Reflection:

- Where did I lead by serving others this week?

- What challenged me about showing up with intention?
- How did service impact my team or school culture?
- Where do I want to keep growing next week?

WEEK 32:

MENTORING AND ENCOURAGING COLLEAGUES

"In a culture of love, we lift each other higher through encouragement, support, and shared wisdom."

Discuss:

- What does mentoring look like in a staff environment—formally or informally?

- What impact does encouragement have on a colleague's confidence or growth?

- Who has encouraged or mentored you in your teaching or leadership journey?

Learn:

Mentoring isn't just a formal role—it's a mindset. Every staff member has the ability to encourage, support, and offer guidance to someone else. Whether it's through shared planning, a conversation in the staffroom, or feedback after a hard day, mentoring happens when we choose to show up for each other with empathy and belief.

Healthy mentoring means we:

- Offer encouragement without fixing
- Share what we've learned without superiority
- Ask questions and listen deeply
- Celebrate others' wins as if they're our own
- Create a safe place for growth, not performance

In strong teams, encouragement isn't rare—it's part of the culture.

Demonstrate:

Create a 'Pass the Torch' moment. Bring a small LED candle or a handmade paper torch. Begin by sharing one encouraging observation about a colleague in the room—a strength, a recent win, or something you admire.

Then pass the torch to that person. They must now do the same—offering genuine encouragement to someone else before passing it on.

Leader Share:

As the host, share a story of a time when someone mentored or encouraged you in a way that made a lasting difference. What did they do or say that stuck with you? How has it shaped how you now encourage others?

Our School Statement:

Together, write your school statement for the week.

For example: *"In this school, we build each other up through mentoring and encouragement."*

In this school,

Connect Groups:

- Share a time when someone's encouragement helped you grow or persevere.
- What does everyday mentoring look like in our school setting?
- How can we create more space for encouragement and support this week?

My Goal This Week:

Write one small, specific action you can take to mentor or encourage someone this week.

Personal Growth Reflection:

- Where did I mentor or encourage someone well this week?
- What challenged me about supporting others?
- How did encouragement shape our staff culture or relationships?
- Where do I want to keep growing next week?

WEEK 33:

PRIORITISING SUCCESS— MANAGING WHAT MATTERS MOST

"In a culture of love, we focus our energy on what matters most—not just what shouts the loudest."

Discuss:

- What does prioritising well look like in a healthy staff culture?
- What distracts us from focusing on what really matters?
- How do our priorities shape our team's success and well-being?

Learn:

It's easy to get caught up in the urgent and overlook the important. But real success doesn't come from doing more—it comes from doing what matters most with purpose. Prioritising well helps us protect our energy, serve our students and teams better, and lead ourselves with clarity.

Healthy prioritisation includes:

- Knowing your values and letting them shape your choices
- Creating space for what's truly important, not just what's loudest
- Saying yes to what aligns with your purpose, and no to what doesn't
- Supporting each other to stay focused, not overwhelmed
- Remembering that rest, clarity, and boundaries are part of success

When we model this kind of prioritisation, we help create a culture of sustainable success.

Demonstrate:

Bring two empty jars and a variety of objects:

- Large stones (labelled with key values: connection, learning, health)
- Smaller pebbles (tasks and meetings)
- Sand (emails, interruptions)
- Water (distractions, noise)

In one jar, pour the water and sand first, then try to fit the pebbles and stones. They don't all fit.

In the second jar, place the big rocks in first, then the pebbles, then the sand—it all fits. Pour a little water last, and the jar still holds everything.

Reflect together:

- What happens when we let the little things take over?
- How does starting with what matters most help everything else fall into place?

Leader Share:

As the host of this session, share a story of a time when you had to realign your priorities in your work or leadership. What shifted when you made space for what mattered most?

Our School Statement:

Together, write your school statement for the week.

For example: *"In this school, we manage what matters most so we can thrive together."*

In this school,

Connect Groups:

- Share a time when prioritising well helped you or your team succeed.
- What do you consider to be your "big rocks" in this season?
- How can we support each other to focus on what matters most this week?

My Goal This Week:

Write one small, specific action you can take to prioritise well this week.

Personal Growth Reflection:

- Where did I prioritise well this week?
- What challenged me about managing my energy or focus?
- How did this impact my relationships or team culture?
- Where do I want to keep growing next week?

WEEK 34:

SOLVING PROBLEMS CREATIVELY AND COLLABORATIVELY

"In a culture of love, we don't avoid problems—we face them together with creativity, courage, and care."

Discuss:

- What helps us solve problems well as a team?
- What gets in the way of collaboration during times of stress or conflict?
- How do creativity and connection shape our ability to find good solutions?

Learn:

Every team will face challenges. What defines a strong culture is not the absence of problems, but how we choose to face them. When we stay connected, curious, and open-minded, we create space for innovative and collaborative solutions.

Creative problem-solving means we:

- Stay calm and connected under pressure
- Value everyone's voice, not just the loudest
- Look for new possibilities rather than recycling blame
- Use humour, flexibility, and perspective to shift stuck thinking
- Trust that we are stronger together

When we combine our strengths and step into problems with courage, the solutions we discover are often better than any one person could have found alone.

Demonstrate:

Place a tray or large plate with 10–20 random items on it (e.g. rubber band, spoon, highlighter, sticky note, magnet, dice, key, button, clothespin, marble, coin, etc.) and cover with a tea towel. Let everyone have 20 seconds to observe the tray in silence before covering it with the tea towel.

Ask staff to silently write down as many items as they can remember.

Next, ask staff to pair up. Allow them a brief 10-second look at the items again, and working together, have them write down as many items as they can remember.

Reveal the answers and celebrate the pair who recalled the most. Observe that when we work together we can achieve more than when we work alone.

Reflect together:

- What helped you remember more as a team?
- How did combining perspectives or noticing different things help?
- How does this relate to solving real-life problems together?

Leader Share:

As the host, share a time when your team had to face a difficult or unexpected challenge and how working together—with a mix of creativity and calm—helped you find a better solution.

Our School Statement:

Together, write your school statement for the week.

For example: *"In this school, we solve problems creatively and collaboratively."*

In this school,

Connect Groups:

- Share a time when working with others helped you see a solution you hadn't thought of.
- What habits help us stay collaborative in times of pressure?
- What's one area where creative teamwork could help this week?

My Goal This Week:

Write one small, specific action you can take to solve problems collaboratively this week.

Personal Growth Reflection:

- Where did I contribute to creative or collaborative problem-solving this week?

- What challenged me about working through a problem with others?

- How did it impact our team or school culture?

- Where do I want to keep growing next week?

WEEK 35:

EMPOWERING OTHERS TO OWN THEIR CHOICES

"In a culture of love, we support others without taking over—because ownership builds confidence, growth, and responsibility."

Discuss:

- What does it mean to truly empower someone in our staff culture?

- What's the difference between supporting someone and rescuing them?

- What happens when we take ownership away from others, even with good intentions?

Learn:

Empowerment is not about doing things for others—it's about equipping them to do it themselves. In strong staff cultures, we believe in each other's capacity, and we resist the urge to take over, fix, or control. Empowering others builds ownership, courage, and long-term growth.

Empowering someone includes:

- Listening without jumping to solutions
- Asking curious questions that spark reflection
- Sharing tools and insight without pressure
- Holding space for others to rise
- Celebrating effort, not just outcomes

When we empower instead of rescue, we communicate: "You've got this—and I've got your back."

Demonstrate:

Bring two bags or containers. One is labelled "Empower," the other "Rescue."

Inside the Rescue bag, place items like:

- A whistle (taking control)
- Sticky tape (trying to hold things together for others)
- An eraser (wiping away mistakes for someone)
- A cape (hero mentality)

Inside the Empower bag, include:

- A mirror (self-reflection)
- A compass (guidance, not direction)

- A pen (writing their own next step)
- A cheer flag or pom-pom (celebration)

Briefly describe each item and ask:

- Which bag are we drawing from more often?
- What shifts when we choose to empower over rescue?

Leader Share:

As the host, share a story of a time when you resisted the urge to take over and instead empowered a student or colleague to take ownership. What happened? How did it strengthen your relationship or their growth?

Our School Statement:

Together, write your school statement for the week.

For example: *"In this school, we empower each other to take ownership and grow with confidence."*

In this school,

Connect Groups:

- Share a time when someone empowered you instead of rescuing you. What made it meaningful?
- Where are we tempted to take over instead of support?
- What can we do to empower one another in our team this week?

My Goal This Week:

Write one small, specific action you can take to empower others this week.

Personal Growth Reflection:

- Where did I practise empowering someone well this week?
- What challenged me about stepping back and trusting others?
- How did empowerment impact our staff culture or relationships?
- Where do I want to keep growing next week?

WEEK 36:

HEALTHY BOUNDARIES FOR SUSTAINABLE LEADERSHIP

*"In a culture of love, boundaries protect what matters most—
our well-being, our relationships, and our purpose."*

Discuss:

- What do healthy boundaries look like in our professional lives?

- What makes it hard to hold or communicate boundaries at work?

- How do clear boundaries protect both connection and sustainability?

Learn:

Leadership without boundaries quickly becomes burnout. Boundaries are not barriers—they're clear, respectful limits that help us lead from a place of health. When we honour our capacity, protect our priorities, and communicate clearly, we lead with integrity and strength.

Healthy boundaries:

- Communicate clearly what's okay and what's not okay
- Help us avoid resentment, over-functioning, and confusion
- Allow others to take responsibility for their part
- Create environments where everyone knows how to thrive
- Model sustainability and respect in action

Boundaries are a gift—to ourselves, and to those we lead.

Demonstrate:

Bring a small container (e.g. a student's pencil case) and a collection of random items—more than can fit inside. Try to cram everything in quickly. Items spill out, the container won't shut, and it becomes a mess.

Then try again—this time choosing just a few essential items. It fits, it closes, and it's manageable.

Ask:

- What are we trying to carry that doesn't actually fit?
- What would it look like to set a clear boundary for what we will and won't carry this week?

Leader Share:

As the host, share a time when setting or honouring a boundary helped you lead more sustainably. Or, reflect on a time when a lack of boundaries led to overload—and what you learned from that experience.

143

Our School Statement:

Together, write your school statement for the week.

For example: *"In this school, we honour healthy boundaries to lead with clarity, purpose, and care."*

In this school,

Connect Groups:

- Share a time when a boundary helped you protect your well-being or purpose.
- Where do we need clearer boundaries in our team culture?
- What boundary will help you lead well this week?

My Goal This Week:

Write one small, specific action you can take to set healthy boundaries this week.

Personal Growth Reflection:

- Where did I practise setting or respecting boundaries this week?
- What challenged me about communicating or holding those boundaries?
- How did this impact my leadership, energy, or relationships?
- Where do I want to keep growing next week?

WEEK 37:

CELEBRATING SUCCESSES AND MILESTONES TOGETHER

*"In a culture of love, we pause to recognise growth,
effort, and the moments that matter––because
celebration builds connection."*

Discuss:

- Why is celebration important in a staff culture?
- What kinds of success are worth recognising—and how do we define them?
- What happens when we skip past wins without acknowledging them?

Learn:

Celebration isn't just for big achievements—it's for the daily wins, the unseen effort, the personal progress, and the team milestones. Taking time to pause and honour these moments builds morale, connection, and a shared sense of purpose.

Celebration doesn't have to be loud or formal. It can be:

- A thank-you note or kind word
- A quick moment of applause at a meeting
- A post-it on a colleague's desk
- A morning tea, a shared laugh, or a group high five
- A moment of stillness to simply say, "We did that."

When we celebrate together, we remind each other that what we do—and how we grow—matters.

Demonstrate:

Before the session, ask staff to email or write down one thing they've noticed a colleague do well this term. Collect these and randomly read out a few (keeping them anonymous if preferred). Then invite the team to join in a "One Clap Celebration" for each one—just one loud, joyful clap in unison.

It's quick, it's light-hearted—and it reinforces that wins, big or small, are worth noticing.

Leader Share:

As the host, share a time when being recognised, even in a small way, meant more to you than expected. What impact did it have? Or share a story of when your team stopped to celebrate something, and how that moment strengthened your culture.

Our School Statement:

Together, write your school statement for the week.

For example: *"In this school, we celebrate growth, success, and each other—because every step forward matters."*

In this school,

Connect Groups:

- Share something you're proud of from this term––big or small.
- What helps you feel genuinely seen and appreciated at work?
- How can we bring more celebration into our everyday culture?

My Goal This Week:

Write one small, specific action you can take to celebrate others this week.

Personal Growth Reflection:

- What did I celebrate in myself or others this week?
- What challenged me about recognising success or slowing down to notice growth?
- How did celebration impact our staff culture or connection?
- Where do I want to keep growing next week?

WEEK 38:

ENCOURAGING GROWTH IN OTHERS—INVESTING BEYOND YOURSELF

"In a culture of love, leadership means lifting others, not just leading them."

Discuss:

- What does it look like to encourage growth in a colleague?
- Who has believed in you or invested in your growth—and what impact did it have?
- Why is it important to invest in others, even when we're busy?

Learn:

Encouraging growth in others is one of the most powerful and generous things we can do as professionals. It's not about having all the answers—it's about noticing potential, calling it out, and creating space for others to rise.

Investing in others looks like:

- Offering encouragement before they think they're ready
- Asking questions that spark reflection and self-belief
- Sharing tools, resources, or feedback with kindness
- Holding space for risk-taking, mistakes, and wins
- Celebrating progress—even the parts we didn't shape

When we invest beyond ourselves, we build a culture where leadership is multiplied, not hoarded—and where success is shared.

Demonstrate:

Bring in a potted plant and a small watering can. Explain that the plant doesn't grow because you pull on it, or because you stand over it and demand results. It grows because you consistently tend to it—water, light, time, and care.

Hold up the watering can and say:

"Encouraging growth in others is like watering this plant. You might not see results immediately. You might wonder if it's working. But over time, the investment shows."

Then hold up a second plant that's been neglected (real or artificial).

"When we overlook the potential in others—not because of ill intent, but simply because we're too busy—we miss the opportunity to help them thrive."

What does it look like to water the potential of the people around you?

Leader Share:

As the host, share a story of someone who encouraged your growth before you believed in yourself. What did they say or do that made the difference? How does it influence the way you now invest in others?

Our School Statement:

Together, write your school statement for the week.

For example: *"In this school, we encourage growth in each other and invest beyond ourselves."*

In this school,

Connect Groups:

- Share a time when someone encouraged your growth.
- Who might be ready for encouragement, trust, or a leadership opportunity this term?
- How can we invest in each other this week in practical ways?

My Goal This Week:

Write one small, specific action you can take to invest in others this week.

Personal Growth Reflection:

- Where did I encourage or invest in someone else this week?
- What challenged me about making time or space for others' growth?
- How did this impact our team culture or connection?
- Where do I want to keep growing next week?

WEEK 39:

HANDLING DISAPPOINTMENT WITH STRENGTH AND PERSPECTIVE

"In a culture of love, we respond to disappointment with honesty, strength, and a willingness to keep growing."

Discuss:

- What does disappointment look like in our work?
- How do we usually respond—inwardly or outwardly—when things don't go to plan?
- What helps us move through disappointment without getting stuck?

Learn:

Disappointment is part of every leadership journey—projects don't land, people let us down, or things shift unexpectedly. But how we respond to these moments matters. Disappointment doesn't have to derail us—it can develop us.

Healthy responses to disappointment include:

- Acknowledging what we hoped for, and why it mattered
- Naming the emotions honestly, without shame
- Looking for perspective—what's still true and possible?
- Choosing growth over bitterness or blame
- Supporting each other through the valleys, not just the wins

When we model healthy disappointment, we show our teams and students how to stay powerful even when things feel hard.

Demonstrate:

Place a deflated balloon on a table alongside a full one. Hold up the full balloon—it represents hope, excitement, or plans.

Now pop or deflate it (dramatically, but safely!). Say: "This is what disappointment can feel like—deflating, loud, even a little shocking."

Then show a balloon pump or a new balloon:

"What helps us recover is not pretending it didn't happen—but choosing to slowly reinflate what matters: perspective, purpose, and resilience."

Leader Share:

As the host, share a time when you experienced disappointment at work—maybe a missed opportunity, a rough season, or something that didn't go as planned. What helped you move through it with strength and perspective?

Our School Statement:

Together, write your school statement for the week.

For example: *"In this school, we handle disappointment with honesty, strength, and hope."*

In this school,

Connect Groups:

- Share a time when disappointment challenged you—and what helped you grow from it.
- What small practices or mindsets help you bounce back after setbacks?
- How can we support each other through disappointment this term?

My Goal This Week:

Write one small, specific action you can take to respond to disappointment well this week.

Personal Growth Reflection:

- Where did I face disappointment this week, and how did I respond?
- What challenged me about staying hopeful or present?
- How did my response affect my well-being, team, or culture?
- Where do I want to keep growing next week?

WEEK 40:

NURTURING A CULTURE OF LOVE

"In a culture of love, we take time to notice how far we've come—and let that shape how we move forward."

Discuss:

- Where have you seen growth in yourself this year?
- Where have you seen growth in our team or school culture?
- Why is it important to pause and celebrate progress?

Learn:

Growth doesn't always look like a big transformation. Sometimes it's subtle—a mindset shift, a repaired relationship, a moment of courage, or simply showing up when things were hard. When we celebrate growth, we remind ourselves that every step forward matters.

Nurturing a culture of love means:

- Recognising effort, not just outcomes
- Making space to reflect, not just race forward
- Sharing wins, even when they feel small
- Valuing the journey, not just the finish line
- Letting growth inspire hope for what's next

When we celebrate growth—in ourselves, our students, and each other — we fuel the culture we want to build.

Demonstrate:

Bring a large poster titled **"Culture of Love."** Invite each staff member to write down one moment of growth they've observed this year on a sticky note. These could include:

- A staff member who spoke up
- A team that pulled together
- Someone who led with courage
- A shift in how challenges were faced
- Parents picking up on the language and approach

Read 3–5 aloud, then invite staff to silently read more after the session.

Say:

"These moments might not have made the newsletter. But they mattered. Together, they've shaped who we are becoming—and the culture we're building."

Leader Share:

As the host, share a personal reflection on growth you've witnessed this year—in yourself, in a colleague, or across the school culture as a whole. What surprised you? What encouraged you? What are you hopeful for going forward?

Our School Statement:

Together, write your school statement for the week.

For example: *"In this school, we celebrate growth—because every step forward shapes our future."*

In this school,

Whole Group Reflection Activity 1: In a Culture of Love...

Before the session:

- Print or display the full list of "Culture of Love Statements" located at the back of this book or on our website (www. godwinconsulting.com.au) as a printable poster or desk flip.

During the session:

Invite each staff member to silently read through the 40 "Culture of Love..." statements. Ask them to highlight or note down the 1–2 statements that most resonated with them this year.

Then go around the circle and invite each person to share:

- Which statement stood out to them and how it was impactful

Encourage celebration and storytelling—this is a chance to honour personal growth and the collective journey.

Whole Group Reflection Activity 2: In This School…

Before the session:

- Create a finalised version of your school's collective "In this school…" statements—one for each week
- Print a copy for each staff member and prepare a large poster to display

During the session:

Invite everyone to look back through their own books and find their weekly "In this school…" statements, reflecting on how their perspectives have grown.

Say:

"These 40 statements represent the culture we've built together—week by week, conversation by conversation."

Then, ask everyone to stand and, on the count of three, read aloud the school's finalised 40 "In this school…" statements together, in unison—a celebration of shared purpose and progress.

Pause and let the moment settle.

Then say:

"This is the sound of a culture of love—not one voice, but many. Not one rulebook, but shared purpose. Not perfection, but progress, owned by all of us."

My Goal This Week:

Write one small, meaningful action you can take to celebrate someone else's growth this week.

Personal Growth Reflection:

- Where did I notice or celebrate growth this week?
- What challenged me about pausing to reflect?
- How has my mindset, behaviour, or leadership shifted this year?
- What do I want to carry forward into the next season?

BONUS TOPICS

Extra sessions for the weeks that stretch a little longer—or when your team is ready to go a little deeper.

Think of this Bonus Section as some extra goodness for those weeks when the term runs a little longer than usual—or when you've got space during professional development days, twilight sessions, or staff retreats.

These sessions are designed to build on everything your team has already explored, offering opportunities to go deeper, reflect further, and strengthen your staff culture even more. Whether it's diving into topics like personal responsibility, team dynamics, or inclusive leadership, each bonus session offers fresh insights and practical challenges to keep the momentum going.

Use them flexibly. Adapt them for the moment. And enjoy the space to keep growing into the kind of staff culture where people feel empowered, connected, and proud to lead together.

BONUS:

CHOICES AND CONSEQUENCES—
OWNING THE IMPACT OF
OUR DECISIONS

"In a culture of love, we take responsibility for our choices—
because freedom and accountability go hand in hand."

Discuss:

- Why is it important to acknowledge the impact of our choices?
- What happens when we separate freedom from responsibility?
- How does a culture change when people own their decisions?

Learn:

Every choice we make has a ripple effect, for better or worse. In a healthy staff culture, we don't avoid this truth—we embrace it.

Responsibility is not about blame; it's about owning the impact of our decisions and learning from them.

Owning our choices means:

- Acknowledging how our actions affect others
- Being willing to repair, reset, or apologise if needed
- Reflecting before reacting
- Staying empowered rather than making excuses
- Leading ourselves with maturity and care

When people feel safe and supported, they're more likely to own their behaviour and grow through it—not hide from it.

Demonstrate:

Hold up a tube of toothpaste and a blank sheet of paper. Squeeze a large amount of toothpaste onto the paper in a messy, visible swirl.

Then ask:

"Can anyone put the toothpaste back in?"

Wait for responses, then reflect:

"Just like our choices—once something is said or done, we can't always undo it. But we *can* take responsibility. We can clean up the mess, own the impact, and choose to grow from it."

Ask the group:

- What does it look like to "clean up the mess" in a healthy staff culture?

- How does this change the way we respond to mistakes—in ourselves or in others?

Leader Share:

As the host, share a moment when you had to own a choice that didn't land well—even if your intentions were good. What did you learn from taking responsibility for the impact?

Our School Statement:

Together, write your school statement for the week.

For example: *"In this school, we own the impact of our choices and grow through reflection."*

In this school,

Connect Groups:

- Share a time when someone owned their actions and it built trust.
- What helps us take responsibility when we make a mistake?
- How can we support each other to own our decisions well this week?

My Goal This Week:

Write one small, meaningful action you can take to take ownership of your choices this week.

Personal Growth Reflection:

- Where did I take ownership for my choices this week?
- What challenged me about owning impact instead of just intentions?
- How did this affect my relationships or leadership?
- Where do I want to keep growing next week?

Bonus: Setting Personal and Professional Goals

"In a culture of love, we grow on purpose—not by pressure, but with clarity and direction."

Discuss:

- Why is it important to set both personal and professional goals?
- What helps a goal feel purposeful rather than performative?
- How do clear goals affect the way we lead ourselves and support others?

Learn:

Goals give us direction—they turn vague hopes into intentional action. When we set goals with clarity, we build momentum, boost confidence, and take ownership of our growth. A healthy culture supports people to dream, define, and pursue what matters most to them.

Setting meaningful goals means:

- Reflecting on what matters, not just what's urgent
- Balancing challenge with compassion

- Setting clear and achievable steps
- Allowing space for reflection, flexibility, and revision
- Celebrating progress, not just outcomes

When we pursue growth on purpose, we don't just become more pro-
ductive—we become more aligned.

Demonstrate:

Bring a compass and a map (or show an image). Explain:

"Having a goal is like setting a destination on a map. Without it, you
might stay busy, but never really arrive anywhere meaningful."

Ask:

- What happens when we lose sight of the direction we're headed?
- How can checking the "compass" of our values help us set the
  right goals?

Encourage staff to write one **personal** and one **professional** goal they'd
like to focus on in the term ahead—no pressure to share, just to name
what matters.

Leader Share:

As the host, share a personal story about a goal that shaped your
professional journey. What helped you stay focused? What challenged
you? How did it influence your confidence or culture?

Our School Statement:

Together, write your school statement for the week.

For example: *"In this school, we set purposeful goals and support each other to grow."*

In this school,

Connect Groups:

- What's a goal that's inspired or stretched you recently?
- How can we support one another's goals with encouragement and accountability?
- What's one step you can take toward a meaningful goal this week?

My Goal This Week:

Write one small, meaningful action you can take to set and move toward your goals this week.

Personal Growth Reflection:

- Where did I take a step toward my goals this week?
- What challenged me about staying committed or focused?
- How did having clear goals influence my leadership or mindset?
- Where do I want to keep growing next week?

BONUS:

INCLUSION AND DIVERSITY— CREATING A PLACE FOR EVERYONE

"In a culture of love, everyone belongs—not by becoming the same, but by being truly seen, heard, and valued."

Discuss:

- What does genuine inclusion look and feel like in a staff culture?
- What's the difference between being included and feeling like you truly belong?
- How do we honour differences while creating unity?

Learn:

Inclusion is more than a policy—it's a posture. It's the daily decision to make space for every person, story, and perspective. Diversity brings depth, creativity, and strength. But inclusion is what turns that diversity into belonging.

Creating a culture of inclusion means:

- Listening to understand, not just respond
- Making room for multiple ways of thinking, being, and learning
- Checking our own assumptions and biases
- Naming and addressing exclusion when we see it
- Creating shared spaces where difference is not just accepted—it's celebrated

When every staff member feels safe to show up as themselves, the whole team flourishes.

Demonstrate:

Bring in a mixed assortment of chairs (or show photos of them): a beanbag, a plastic chair, a fancy armchair, a stool, a folding chair, a booster seat. Arrange them together in a visible circle.

Say:

"Every chair has a different shape, purpose, and story—just like us. If we were to make room at this table, we wouldn't ask the stool to become an armchair. We'd adjust the table to ensure everyone can reach."

Ask:

- What does it look like to make space for difference in our staff culture?

- Where might someone be sitting in a "chair" that we've over-looked or misunderstood?

Leader Share:

As the host, share a story of when someone made room for your voice or identity, or a time when you witnessed inclusion shift the atmosphere of a team. What was the impact?

Our School Statement:

Together, write your school statement for the week.

For example: *"In this school, everyone belongs—and we create space for difference to be seen and valued."*

In this school,

Connect Groups:

- Share a time when you felt truly included—what made it powerful?
- What do you think is still missing in our culture of inclusion?
- What's one way we can create a stronger sense of belonging this week?

My Goal This Week:

Write one small, meaningful action you can take to include others this week.

Personal Growth Reflection:

- Where did I help someone feel included this week?
- What challenged me about noticing or naming exclusion?
- How did my awareness or actions influence team culture?
- Where do I want to keep growing next week?

BONUS:

NAVIGATING PEER PRESSURE AND TEAM CULTURE DYNAMICS

"In a culture of love, we choose integrity over approval—and lead with courage, not conformity."

Discuss:

- What does peer pressure look like in adult staff culture?
- How do unspoken expectations influence behaviour, language, or participation?
- What helps you stay aligned with your values, even when the group feels off track?

Learn:

Peer pressure doesn't disappear in adulthood—it just becomes more subtle. It can show up as pressure to stay silent, go along with negativity, overwork to keep up, or avoid speaking up when something feels wrong.

Navigating team culture dynamics well means:

- Being aware of the influence we have—and the influence we're under
- Choosing honesty over passive agreement
- Refusing to participate in gossip, exclusion, or toxic humour
- Speaking up with care when something compromises the culture we're building
- Remembering that integrity is quiet leadership—and it matters

Healthy staff cultures are built when individuals choose to model what they value, even when it's hard.

Demonstrate:

Bring a stack of blank labels or name tags. On a few of them, write subtle "pressures" that staff might feel (e.g. "Don't speak up," "Go along with the joke," "Work late = more committed," "Stay neutral," "Be liked, not honest").

Stick these on a volunteer's shirt, one at a time, reading them aloud as you do.

Say:

"These are the invisible messages that shape our culture—often without us realising. They weigh us down and shrink our freedom."

Then invite others to name what mindsets or messages they've had to peel off in order to stay aligned with their values. Remove the stickers one by one, as a visual act of reclaiming authenticity and leadership.

Leader Share:

As the host, share a time when you felt pressure to conform to team dynamics—and how you chose (or wished you had chosen) to stay aligned with your values instead. What happened? What did you learn?

Our School Statement:

Together, write your school statement for the week.

For example: "In this school, we lead with integrity, even when it's uncomfortable—because culture is everyone's responsibility."

In this school,

Connect Groups:

- Share a time when you felt pressure to go along with something that didn't align with your values.
- What helped (or could have helped) you make a different choice?
- What's one way we can support each other to lead with integrity this week?

My Goal This Week:

Write one small, meaningful action you can take to stay aligned with your values this week.

Personal Growth Reflection:

- Where did I choose integrity over conformity this week?
- What challenged me about peer or team dynamics?
- How did my actions influence our culture or relationships?
- Where do I want to keep growing next week?

CULTURE OF LOVE STATEMENTS

7. In a culture of love, listening means creating space for every voice to matter.

8. In a culture of love, feedback means we care enough to speak the truth and listen with humility.

9. In a culture of love, empathy means we seek to understand before we respond.

10. In a culture of love, kindness means using our words to build, not break.

11. In a culture of love, solving problems means working together with honesty, respect, and creativity.

12. In a culture of love, respect means treating every person with value, dignity, and care.

13. In a culture of love, together means we value connection over isolation and teamwork over competition.

14. In a culture of love, trust means showing up consistently with honesty, integrity, and care.

15. In a culture of love, responsibility means owning my actions while staying connected in relationship.

16. In a culture of love, friendship means we champion one another and help each other grow.

17. In a culture of love, ownership means taking responsibility for my choices, my attitude, and my contribution to this workplace.

18. In a culture of love, powerful people lead themselves well, take ownership of their actions, and create space for others to thrive.

19. In a culture of love, we choose connection over control, love over fear, and people over problems.

20. In a culture of love, boundaries protect what matters most and create clarity for healthy connection.

21. In a culture of love, respect means valuing every person, every role, and every story.

22. In a culture of love, every person plays a part in creating and protecting a healthy workplace culture.

23. In a culture of love, mistakes are seen as opportunities for learning, growth, and restoration.

24. In a culture of love, growth happens best in community—where we encourage, challenge, and support one another.

25. In a culture of love, consistency builds trust, creates safety, and sustains culture even when things are hard.

26. In a culture of love, responsibility is not a burden—it's a privilege that brings joy, purpose, and growth.

27. In a culture of love, an apology is not about blame or shame—it's about ownership, restoration, and reconnection.

28. In a culture of love, forgiveness is a choice to let go of offence so we can move forward with freedom and connection.

29. In a culture of love, trust is rebuilt through honesty, humility, and consistent action over time.

30. In a culture of love, second chances create space for growth, learning, and restoration.

31. In a culture of love, taking responsibility builds trust, respect, and personal integrity.

32. In a culture of love, powerful friendships are built on trust, honesty, and respect—not control or dependence.

33. In a culture of love, powerful people take responsibility for themselves, bring safety to others, and lead with respect no matter where they are.

34. In a culture of love, we treat ourselves with the same value, care, and responsibility we extend to others.

35. In a culture of love, we take ownership for what we see and step up with empathy, courage, and care.

36. In a culture of love, we model the kind of people and professionals we hope others will become.

37. In a culture of love, leadership is not about position—it's about choosing to serve with intention and heart.

38. In a culture of love, we lift each other higher through encouragement, support, and shared wisdom.

39. In a culture of love, we focus our energy on what matters most—not just what shouts the loudest.

40. In a culture of love, we don't avoid problems—we face them together with creativity, courage, and care.

41. In a culture of love, we support others without taking over—because ownership builds confidence, growth, and responsibility.

42. In a culture of love, boundaries protect what matters most—our well-being, our relationships, and our purpose.

43. In a culture of love, we pause to recognise growth, effort, and the moments that matter—because celebration builds connection.

44. In a culture of love, leadership means lifting others, not just leading them.

45. In a culture of love, we respond to disappointment with honesty, strength, and a willingness to keep growing.

46. In a culture of love, we take time to notice how far we've come—and let that shape how we move forward.

47. In a culture of love, we take responsibility for our choices—because freedom and accountability go hand in hand.

48. In a culture of love, we grow on purpose—not by pressure, but with clarity and direction.

49. In a culture of love, everyone belongs—not by becoming the same, but by being truly seen, heard, and valued.

50. In a culture of love, we choose integrity over approval—and lead with courage, not conformity.

EQUIPPING STAFF TEAMS FOR A CULTURE OF LOVE AND CONNECTION

At Godwin Consulting, we partner with schools to build strong, sustainable staff cultures rooted in connection, responsibility, and restoration. Whether you're looking to strengthen team dynamics, embed the *LoSoP Culture Series*, or grow your leadership impact, we're here to support your journey.

Our tailored Professional Development sessions, LoSoP Coaching, and personalised Key Leader Consultations are designed to help staff teams deepen their understanding and confidently apply the *LoSoP* principles. These practical experiences equip you to:

- Lead from any role—with integrity, intention, and compassion
- Create staff cultures grounded in joy, clarity, and meaningful relationships
- Build strong classroom cultures by modelling powerful staffroom connection
- Raise up leaders who multiply culture, not just manage behaviour

To support ongoing learning, we also offer:

The LoSoP Foundations Online Course

A flexible, self-paced introduction to the key principles of *Loving Our Students On Purpose*. Perfect for onboarding new staff or building a shared foundation across your whole team.

The Neuroscience of Connection Course

Dive deeper into the "why" behind LoSoP. This professional learning experience explores the brain-body-behaviour connection, trauma-informed practice, and the science that underpins emotional safety, regulation, and relational leadership.

The LoSoP Team Trainer Program

Looking to embed this work long-term? Identify and equip key staff as in-house LoSoP trainers. This program provides the tools, mentoring, and structure needed to lead LoSoP in your staffroom and sustain momentum school-wide.

With our expertise in behaviour education, organisational culture, and leadership development, we'll help you create a school where every staff member feels seen, valued, and supported—and where the culture you carry transforms every boardroom, staffroom and classroom.

Visit www.godwinconsulting.com.au to:

- Book your next professional development session
- Enrol in the *LoSoP Foundations* or *Neuroscience of Connection* online courses

- Discuss our Key Leader Consult professional conversations
- Launch the *LoSoP Team Trainer Program* in your school

Together, let's build a staff culture where love leads, connection grows, and leadership is shared by all.

ABOUT THE AUTHOR

Bernii Godwin holds a Master's qualification in Social Work and a Graduate Certificate in Neuropsychotherapy, building on her under-graduate degree in Human Services and Criminology and Criminal Justice, with a focus on youth and family justice. She is also a certi-fied Loving on Purpose Trainer and John Maxwell Leadership Team Member.

Over the past two decades, Bernii has worked in various roles across a wide range of schools, specialising in student well-being and be-haviour. Principals frequently seek her expertise to consult on complex behaviour and well-being issues, provide one-on-one coaching or supervision to educators and well-being teams, and deliver school-wide professional development. Her greatest passion is helping schools adopt practical tools that replace fear and punishment with purposeful behaviour education, safe connections, and empowered teachers—ul-timately increasing student engagement in their academic journey.

To connect with Bernii, please visit

www.godwinconsulting.com.au